FIX
ME
A
PLATE

FIX ME A PLATE

Traditional and
New School
Soul Food Recipes
from Scotty Scott
of Cook Drank Eat

SCOTTY SCOTT

PAGE STREET
PUBLISHING CO.

PAGE STREET
PUBLISHING CO.

First published in 2021 by
Page Street Publishing Co.
27 Congress Street, Suite 1511
Salem, MA 01970
www.pagestreetpublishing.com

Distributed by Macmillan, sales in Canada by The Canadian Manda Group.

26   25   24   23   22   1   2   3   4   5

ISBN-13: 978-1-64567-450-4
ISBN-10: 1-64567-450-9

Library of Congress Control Number: 2021931970

Cover and book design by Kylie Alexander for Page Street Publishing Co.
Photography by Scotty Scott and Rambo Elliot

Printed and bound in the United States

DEDICATION

To Mom and Pop. In the kitchen and on the grill, your love of cooking
helped spread joy throughout our family.

CONTENTS

INTRODUCTION

"Scotty! Wake up . . . wake up! The house is on fire!" My father grabbed my nine-year-old hand and yanked me off my parents' bed. Coughing as we rushed to the front door while shielding our eyes from the smoke, I kept thinking to myself, "What in the heck is going on?" As we made our way outside, I saw my mother and older sister looking on in horror as smoke billowed out of the open front door. I could hear the fire engine's siren wailing in the distance as I looked up at my father who was looking down at me in disgust. "What happened?" I asked. "You forgot to cut off the ham hocks and almost burnt the damn house down." "Oh yeah, the ham hocks," I said. My mother, father and older sister had gone shopping and left me at home with explicit instructions to turn off the ham hocks that were boiling on the stove when the timer went off. Easy enough. However, instead of completing this simple task, I grabbed an armful of snacks and climbed in my parents' bed to watch cartoons. Shortly thereafter, I slipped into an ice-cream-and-Cheetos-induced coma, only to be rudely awakened by thick, black smoke, the blaring smoke alarms, the kitchen timer that had been going off for an hour and the vise grip hold of my incredibly disappointed father. Fortunately, there was no fire. Just ham hocks smoldering in a dry pot still set to high. It would be a long-ass time before we got the stench of burnt ham hocks out of our home. It would be equally as long before I was allowed anywhere near the stove again.

From an early age, I always wanted to be involved in the kitchen. From my grandmother frying up hot-water cornbread in her cast-iron skillet, to my father grilling up a feast for the whole family on a summer holiday, my best conversations always seemed to be when the food was being prepared. My mother worked two jobs and my father odd hours, which meant that oftentimes, I was left to fend for myself for dinner. Around twelve years old, tired of me complaining about eating frozen dinners or leftovers, my parents finally agreed to let me put my chef coat back on. It started slowly . . . steaming veggies, maybe frying up a burger, but eventually, it became whole meals for both me and my family. Although, over the years, I was frequently asked by friends and family when I was going to write a cookbook or open a restaurant, I never really saw food as a career path. My mother, a high school guidance counselor for 40 years, always reiterated that I needed to get a college degree and find a good, stable job. So off to college and then law school I went. It wasn't until I graduated law school and began hosting dinner parties that I decided to take cooking a bit more seriously.

After starting a personal chef service, I decided to dabble in social media a bit to promote the business. What I discovered at that point would probably be best described as life changing. Growing up, I was the class clown. I would write ridiculous stories that had my classmates (and many times, the teacher) laughing hysterically. For some reason though, I never considered writing, or any creative outlet for that matter, as a career option. I was always looking to create and be creative but could not find my niche. My voice is terrible, my dance moves are Elaine Benes-esque and my drawings look like I probably used my foot. However, that changed when I found social media, wherein I was able to combine two passions: cooking and photography. In order to set yourself apart and gain a following on social media, you have to be creative, and you have to stay creative, which I embraced both with my recipes and cooking videos. My goal has always been to make my cooking tutorials both informative and entertaining in an attempt to avoid the monotony of step 1, 2, 3 cooking videos.

My hope is that in this book you will not only learn new recipes and possibly cooking techniques but also get a close look into my creative process and cooking style. As with my cooking videos, this should be a guide for cooking ideas and cooking as an expression of creativity. My recipes are meant to be a starting point whereby you are able to add your own flair and personal touch to whatever you are cooking. They begin with an energy, a mindset and a vision that guide me through the process, and hopefully these recipes do the same for you. The photos and recipes herein are an insight into that vision and culinary vibe.

MORNIN'

One thing I love about soul food breakfasts is that there are no rules. Any kind of protein, paired with any kind of carb (a lot of times it's grits) . . . as long as it's good and hearty and will get you through the day. Because let's face it, grown folks cannot subsist on flapjacks alone. One of my favorite recipes and one of the more quintessential soul food breakfast items is the biscuit. The biscuit is to Southern cooking as the bagel is to a New York deli. Rare is the bread that can break free of being a side item and become a meal in and of itself, but add a little bit (or a lotta bit) of gravy as in my Southern Raised Biscuits with Spicy Sausage Cream Gravy (page 12) and you've got just that. Another favorite is the Catfish and Grits (page 16). As someone who doesn't eat pork (or eggs, but that's a story for another day, see page 90), I'm always searching for a breakfast protein. Hearty and delicious, many times this was the leftover catfish from Friday night's fish fry paired with some delicious grits for a great and satisfying breakfast.

SOUTHERN RAISED BISCUITS WITH SPICY SAUSAGE CREAM GRAVY

Biscuits. Glorious, glorious, light and fluffy biscuits. Unfortunately, my lack of pig participation meant I'd missed out on some pork recipes that I had not been introduced to until after I'd sworn off the swine. (For the full story behind that decision, see page 90.) Sausage gravy was one such dish. I hadn't really paid much attention to it until I accidentally got ahold of some a few years ago. It. Was. Incredible! Unfortunately, bubble guts ensued shortly thereafter. Determined to enjoy this delicious breakfast without my body betraying me, I decided to make my own pork-free sausage, which is actually fairly easy and can be made ahead of time and frozen. You can use straight ground pork or whatever mix you want. In my last batch, I used bison, lamb and elk. The bison is a bit richer than ground beef, and the lamb and elk give it a nice gamey undertone. Feel free to play around with your meat selection to suit your own taste; however, I would not use just beef, as I've found that it just ends up tasting like a spicy hamburger.

For the Sausage (see Note)

3 lbs (1.5 kg) ground meat (choose your own adventure)

2 tbsp (13 g) black pepper

2 tsp (12 g) salt

1 tsp garlic powder

½ tsp cayenne pepper

2 tsp (3 g) paprika

½ tsp crushed red pepper flakes

1 tsp chopped fresh rosemary

2 tsp (1 g) chopped fresh thyme

2 tsp (1 g) chopped fresh sage

1 tbsp (14 g) brown sugar

¼ tsp fennel

For the Biscuits

2¾ cups (624 g) unsalted butter

2 (½-oz [7-g]) envelopes active dry yeast

¼ cup (60 ml) warm water

5 cups (625 g) all-purpose flour

⅓ cup (66 g) granulated sugar

1½ tbsp (21 g) baking powder

1 tsp baking soda

1¼ tsp (7 g) salt

2¼ cups (540 ml) cold buttermilk, divided

To make the sausage, in a large bowl, combine the ground meat, pepper, salt, garlic powder, cayenne, paprika, pepper flakes, rosemary, thyme, sage, brown sugar and fennel and mix together to combine with your hands. Yes, you can use a spoon; however, this is most effectively done with your hands. If the thought grosses you out, wear gloves, look away and think happy thoughts. Place the mixture in a large skillet over medium-high heat. Cook for 8 to 9 minutes, or until browned, stirring occasionally and breaking up the large chunks. Remove from the heat, drain and set aside.

To make the biscuits, cut the butter into 1-inch (2.5-cm) cubes and place in the freezer. In a small bowl, combine the yeast and warm water and give it a little stir to combine. Set it aside while preparing the other stuff, 'bout 5 minutes or until bubbly. In a large bowl, whisk the flour, sugar, baking powder, baking soda and salt. Remove the butter from the freezer and cut it into the dry ingredients with a fork until the mixture resembles a coarse meal. Add 2 cups (480 ml) of the buttermilk and the yeast mixture to the dry ingredients and butter, mixing with a fork until the dry ingredients are, dare I say, moistened. Turn the dough onto a floured surface and lightly get your knead on three or four times. Cut the dough in half. Roll out each half until it is 1 inch (2.5 cm) thick. Cut the dough with a biscuit cutter (or mug, Mason jar or whatever you wanna use) dusted with flour and place on a lightly greased baking pan. Cover and let rise for 1 hour. Then, place the pan in the refrigerator for at least 1 hour.

For the Gravy

½ cup (114 g) butter

½ cup (63 g) all-purpose flour

3 cups (720 ml) milk, plus extra if needed

Salt and pepper, to taste

Melted butter, for serving

Preheat the oven to 450°F (230°C).

Remove the biscuits from the refrigerator and brush with the remaining buttermilk, making sure just to dab the tops of the biscuits. The bottoms of the biscuits will burn if you use too much and the buttermilk runs down the sides. Bake the biscuits on the middle rack in the oven for 10 to 12 minutes, or until the tops are golden brown, rotating halfway through. While the biscuits are baking, begin making the gravy.

To make the gravy, in a small saucepan, melt the butter over medium-low heat. Add the flour and whisk to combine. Slowly add the milk and whisk to incorporate. Keep whisking for 1 minute, or until smooth. If the gravy appears too thick add a bit more milk. Add ½ pound (226 g) of the sausage and stir to combine. Add salt and pepper to taste. Keep warm on low heat until the biscuits are done, stirring occasionally and making sure it doesn't burn.

Remove the biscuits from the oven and brush with melted butter. Serve with the sausage gravy. Congrats! You just made biscuits and gravy!

NOTE: This recipe makes 3 pounds (1.5 kg) of sausage. Freeze the leftovers for up to 3 months.

SWEET POTATO BREAD

I call this soul food's answer to banana bread. As the sweet potatoes are not quite as dense as bananas, the result is a deliciously light and fluffy breakfast cake. A light slather of the cinnamon honey butter and you'll be fighting over the last slice.

If you haven't noticed after reading through the Table of Contents, sweet potatoes make quite a few appearances in this book. And for several good reasons! Reason number one, I like sweet potatoes, dammit. Reason number two, which to be honest is actually reason number one, is that sweet potatoes have a long history in Southern cooking. While pumpkins and other gourds are easier to grow in the North, sweet potatoes are more plentiful in the South. In the antebellum South, slave cabins rarely had the cooking equipment or appliances necessary to adequately bake a pie; however, making the desserts in the Big House was often tasked to enslaved African American cooks, and it was through their expertise that sweet potato pie and sweet potatoes in general entered black culture. While not originating in Africa, like okra, sweet potatoes still hold an important place in the hierarchy of soul food ingredients.

2 sweet potatoes

1 cup (200 g) granulated sugar

½ cup (114 g) unsalted butter, room temperature

2 large eggs

1 tsp vanilla extract

1 tbsp (15 ml) milk

½ tsp ground cinnamon

½ tsp ground nutmeg

2 cups (250 g) sifted all-purpose flour

1 tsp baking powder

1 tsp baking soda

1 tsp salt

Cinnamon Honey Butter (page 136)

Preheat the oven to 400°F (200°C).

Slice the sweet potatoes in half long ways, and place them skin side down on a baking sheet. Bake for 15 minutes. Using a spatula, turn them over and bake for another 15 minutes. The tops should be browned, and they should easily be pierced with a fork. Remove the potatoes from the oven and let cool. Slice or peel off the thin flat side of the browned sweet potato and discard. Scoop out the insides and set aside to let cool.

Reduce the oven temperature to 325°F (165°C) and butter a 9 x 5 x 3–inch (23 x 13 x 8–cm) loaf pan.

In a bowl, use an electric mixer to cream the sugar and butter until light and fluffy. Add the eggs, one at a time, beating well after each addition. Add the vanilla and mix till combined. Set aside.

In a small bowl, mash the sweet potatoes with a fork and mix in the milk, cinnamon and nutmeg. In another bowl, mix together the flour, baking powder, baking soda and salt. Add the sweet potatoes to the creamed butter mixture and stir until combined. Add the dry ingredients, mixing until the flour is incorporated. Pour the batter into a prepared loaf pan and bake for 1 hour, or until a toothpick inserted in the center comes out clean. Set the pan on a cooling rack for 15 minutes. Remove the bread from the pan and invert it onto a cooling rack to cool completely before slicing. Serve with my Cinnamon Honey Butter.

CATFISH AND GRITS

You know, I was a bit surprised when I first posted a recipe for catfish and grits by how many people had never heard of this combination. I mean catfish is one of the most popular fish in Southern cooking, and grits, well, everyone knows how folks in the South get down on some grits. One thing I love about this dish is that it's a prime example of how breakfast in the South isn't just eggs and bacon. It's one of those big, hearty meals that could definitely be eaten for dinner but still winds up on the breakfast table when folks are trying to put a serious meal in their bellies to start the day.

For the Catfish

2 cups (480 ml) low-fat buttermilk

2 tbsp (30 ml) hot sauce

6 (7–9-oz [198–255-g]) catfish fillets, rinsed and thoroughly patted dry

1 qt (960 ml) peanut oil

1½ cups (183 g) stone-ground fine cornmeal

1½ cups (188 g) all-purpose flour

2 tsp (4 g) lemon pepper seasoning

2 tsp (5 g) garlic powder

1 tsp onion powder

2 tsp (3 g) paprika

¼ tsp chili powder

⅛ tsp cumin

2 tsp (10 g) kosher salt

½ tsp freshly ground black pepper

For the Grits

2 cups (480 ml) water

2 cups (480 ml) chicken stock

2 cups (312 g) stone-ground grits (I prefer Geechie Boy Mill or Anson Mills)

3 tbsp (42 g) unsalted butter

1 clove garlic, minced

2 cups (226 g) shredded white Cheddar cheese

1 tsp salt

1 cup (240 ml) half-and-half

To make the catfish, in a large bowl, add the buttermilk and hot sauce and mix to combine. Place the catfish fillets in the buttermilk mixture and set aside for 30 minutes.

Heat the peanut oil in a 5-quart (5-L) Dutch oven or fryer over medium heat until it reaches 350°F (180°C) on a deep-fry thermometer.

In a shallow dish, whisk the cornmeal, flour, lemon pepper, garlic powder, onion powder, paprika, chili powder, cumin, salt and pepper. Remove the catfish from the buttermilk mixture and, one at a time, press them into the cornmeal. Flip them over and repeat, making sure to completely coat the fish. Set the coated fillets on a cookie sheet and let them rest for 5 minutes. Gently add the fillets, one or two at a time, to the hot oil and fry until golden brown, 5 to 6 minutes. Remove the fried fillets to a cooling rack or paper towel laid out over a sheet pan.

To make the grits, add the water and chicken stock to a pot and bring to a boil. Whisk in the grits and turn the heat down to low. Simmer, partially covered, until most of the water and stock has been absorbed, about 10 minutes. Place the butter in a small saucepan over low heat to melt (this may also be done in the microwave). Add the garlic to the butter and stir to combine. Add the cheese, salt and garlic butter to the grits and stir to combine. Once the cheese has melted, add the half-and-half and cook for 5 to 10 minutes, or until the grits have thickened a bit and absorbed most of the half-and-half. Remove the grits from the heat.

Serve the catfish atop the hot grits for your delicious Southern breakfast.

YARDBIRD BISCUITS WITH PEPPER PEACH JELLY

YIELD: 6 SERVINGS

This dish begins as most good breakfasts do: with one delicious biscuit. Extremely light, buttery and fluffy, it elicits a Pavlovian response when you break it open. I'd say this is another two-for-one recipe, but this is actually a three-for as each item stands alone on its own delicious merits. I really love this meal, or sandwich, or whatever you want to call this thing because it does a little flavor dance that I love to achieve in my recipes. Savory, with a little bit of sweet and a little bit of heat. Get your biscuit on.

For the Biscuits

6 biscuits (see recipe for Southern Raised Biscuits with Spicy Sausage Cream Gravy [page 12])

For the Chicken

6 boneless, skinless chicken thighs

For the Pepper Peach Jelly

3 tbsp (42 g) unsalted butter

2 fresh jalapeños, sliced

4 cups (650 g) sliced and peeled fresh peaches

½ cup (110 g) brown sugar

¼ cup (50 g) white sugar

¼ tsp salt

½ cup (120 ml) orange juice

Sliced Cheddar cheese, for serving

To make the biscuits, see the recipe on page 12.

To make the chicken, marinate the thighs overnight and prepare as outlined in the Southern Fried Cornish Hens recipe (page 36), replacing the hens with the chicken thighs.

To make the jelly, melt the butter in a small saucepan. Add the jalapeños and cook over medium-low heat for 2 minutes, or until the jalapeños begin to soften. Add the peaches, brown sugar, white sugar, salt and orange juice, and cook over medium-high heat for 25 minutes, stirring occasionally. Remove from the heat and set aside.

To prepare the biscuits, split one biscuit and place a slice of Cheddar on the bottom portion. Place the biscuit under the broiler to melt the cheese. Once the cheese has melted, place a chicken thigh on top of the cheese and top with some of the pepper peach jelly. Place the top of the biscuit on top of the jelly and chicken and enjoy.

BUTTERMILK DROP BISCUITS
WITH BLUEBERRY MINT COMPOTE

One thing I love about this recipe is its simplicity. Drop biscuits are perfect when you don't want to explode that can of shelf biscuits in the fridge but still want that delicious homemade taste. A few simple ingredients and a generous slathering of butter and you've got homemade goodness on your breakfast table. Feel free to create your own variation by adding garlic or even cheese.

For the Blueberry Mint Compote

3 cups (450 g) fresh blueberries

½ cup (110 g) packed brown sugar

2 tsp (10 ml) fresh lemon juice

¼ cup (23 g) chopped fresh mint

¼ tsp salt

½ tsp tapioca

For the Biscuits

1½ cups (188 g) all-purpose flour

1 tbsp (14 g) baking powder

½ tsp kosher salt

1 tsp sugar (optional)

1 large egg

⅔ cup (160 ml) buttermilk

¼ cup (60 ml) melted butter

Preheat the oven to 450°F (230°C). Grease a baking sheet or cast-iron skillet.

To make the compote, wash the blueberries in a colander under cold water, removing any stems. Place them in a small pot over medium-high heat with the brown sugar, lemon juice, mint and salt. Cook for 10 minutes, and then reduce the heat to medium-low and simmer for 5 minutes. Add the tapioca, remove from the heat and set aside. (Note that the consistency will be syrupy but will come together as it sits.)

To make the biscuits, in a large bowl, combine the flour, baking powder, salt and sugar (if using) and whisk to combine. Add the egg, buttermilk and melted butter and stir to mix together.

Using a medium-size spoon, scoop eight portions of dough (2 to 3 table-spoons [30 to 45 g] each) and drop them onto the greased baking sheet or cast-iron skillet. Brush with the buttermilk and place in the oven for 10 to 15 minutes, or until the tops of the biscuits are golden brown. Remove from the oven and brush with melted butter. Serve with the blueberry compote.

SUNDAY WAFFLES

As much as I'd like to think that I'm a pancake dude, if I'm being honest with myself, I'm a waffle guy at heart. There's just something about how the syrup meanders its way through all those different waffle pockets and ridges that just makes waffles hit different. Thanks in part to its partner in brunch crime, fried chicken, there are all kinds of different and new freaky variations of waffles. (For instance, see my Chicken and Brown Butter Sweet Potato Waffles with Maple Bourbon Sauce on page 80.) This is a fairly classic recipe that won't let you down on a lazy Sunday morning.

1 cup (125 g) all-purpose flour

1 cup (125 g) self-rising flour

2 tsp (9 g) baking powder

1 tsp baking soda

¼ tsp salt

1 tbsp (15 g) granulated sugar

3 eggs

4 tbsp (60 ml) melted unsalted butter

2 cups (480 ml) buttermilk, room temperature

1 tsp vanilla extract

Maple syrup, for serving

In a large bowl, sift the all-purpose flour, self-rising flour, baking powder, baking soda, salt and sugar. Separate the egg whites, placing the yolks in one bowl and the whites in another. Beat the egg yolks and add the melted butter, buttermilk and vanilla.

Add the egg yolk mixture to the dry ingredients and beat until smooth. With a hand mixer, beat the egg whites on high until light and fluffy. Gently fold the egg whites into the batter. Pour a spoonful of batter into each section of a waffle iron and cook until browned. Serve with warm maple syrup.

PUT SOME MEAT ON YOUR BONES

When I say that soul food puts some meat on your bones, I mean that both literally and figuratively. Yes, you may very well need a nap after a delicious plate of pork, veggies and carbtastic carbs. But you have also been fed spiritually. You have been fed with recipes that have been passed down from generation to generation. You have been fed with what, in some cases, began as scraps deemed unfit for consumption by some, that now is part of American history, cuisine and culture. This chapter is the meat and potatoes of this book. This is where you'll find dishes that have had hours of love poured into them that you can taste with your first bite. Dishes like Short Rib Grillades (page 32), where the succulent and tender short rib meat is paired with delicious cheese grits and a splash of short rib au jus. Or, one of my personal favorites, Slow and Low Red Beans and Rice (page 26). These slow-cooked beans soak up all the delicious flavors in the pot before getting mashed up a bit to release some of their creamy bean goodness. Whatever your favorite, I'm sure you'll agree these ain't no fancy-pants, pinky-in-the-air finger foods. These are belly- and soul-satisfying meals.

SLOW AND LOW RED BEANS AND RICE

When talking about delicious, nutritious and a little bit that goes a long way, it's hard to beat a big ole pot of beans. And when it comes to beans, red beans and rice is hands down my favorite. While I prefer my black beans crisp and firm, I love to cook down some red beans into a delicious bean slurry. A bit of mashing about three-quarters of the way through the cooking process yields a consistency that's not quite whole bean and not quite refried mash that brings all the textures and flavors of the pot together perfectly.

1 lb (454 g) dried small red beans

1 lb (454 g) andouille or other smoked sausage, cut into ¼" (6-mm) slices

1 tbsp (15 ml) vegetable oil

1 medium yellow onion, chopped

2 celery ribs, chopped

1 green bell pepper, chopped

¼ tsp cayenne pepper

1 tsp salt

½ tsp freshly ground black pepper

4 cloves garlic, minced

2 qt (2 L) chicken broth, divided

1 (15-oz [425-g]) can tomato sauce

1 tsp creole seasoning

2 tbsp (3 g) chopped fresh parsley

½ tsp chopped fresh thyme

3 bay leaves

1 tbsp (15 g) sugar

1 cooked smoked turkey leg, turkey wing or ham hock

3 cups (558 g) cooked white rice

1 tbsp (15 ml) hot sauce

Rinse the beans under cold water in a colander, removing any broken beans or pebbles. Place them in a large pot and cover with water. Bring the beans to a boil, and then shut off the heat and let them rest for 1 hour.

Place the sausage in a large cast-iron skillet or pan and cook over medium-high heat for 5 minutes, until browned, stirring frequently. Remove the sausage using a slotted spoon, leaving the rendered fat in the pan. Add the vegetable oil, onion, celery, bell pepper, cayenne, salt and pepper to the skillet, and sauté for 5 minutes, or until the vegetables start to soften. Add the garlic and cook for 1 minute. Pour the contents of the skillet into a large stockpot.

Add 2 cups (480 ml) of the chicken broth to the skillet to deglaze the pan by scraping the bits from the bottom with a wooden spoon. Pour the contents of the skillet into the stockpot. Add the remaining broth, beans, tomato sauce, creole seasoning, parsley, thyme, bay leaves, sugar and smoked meat, and mix to combine. If the beans are not totally submerged, add water to cover. Bring to a boil, and then reduce the heat to medium-low. Simmer, partially covered, for 2 hours, stirring occasionally. Mash some of the beans against the side of the pot with a heavy spoon to help thicken, and cook for 30 minutes, or until the smoked meat is very tender and beginning to fall off the bone. Remove the bay leaves. Serve in bowls with the prepared rice with a dash of hot sauce.

JUST THE TIPS (BEEF TIPS AND RICE)

This dish is one of those meals that puts soul in your body when you eat it. You just feel the tender meat and flavorful gravy warming you up inside and giving you your soul food superpowers. One such superpower? The ability to take a two-hour nap on the couch in the middle of the day after eating this. This dish is also a pretty good soul food barometer, as well. This means that if you see this on the menu somewhere, disregard the Yelp reviews and get your butt down to that restaurant 'cause chances are they have some soul going on in that kitchen.

For the Meat

2 lbs (907 g) cubed beef stew meat

1 tsp salt, plus more for seasoning

1½ tsp (3 g) freshly ground black pepper, plus more for seasoning

4 tbsp (31 g) all-purpose flour

3 tbsp (45 ml) vegetable or canola oil, plus 1 tbsp (15 ml) if adding mushrooms

2 tbsp (28 g) unsalted butter, plus 2 tbsp (28 g) if adding mushrooms

1 onion, chopped

5 cups (1.2 L) beef stock

1 tsp minced garlic

2 tsp (10 g) onion soup mix

2 tbsp (30 ml) soy sauce

2 tbsp (30 ml) Worcestershire sauce

½ cup (120 ml) water

2 cups (150 g) sliced mushrooms (optional)

Rice, for serving

Generously season the meat with the salt and pepper. Place the flour and meat into a large freezer bag and close. Shake the bag until all of the meat is coated with the flour.

Heat the oil in a large skillet over medium heat. Add the meat and cook for 5 to 6 minutes, or until browned on all sides, stirring frequently. Remove the meat from the pan and set aside.

Add 2 tablespoons (28 g) of the butter to a large pot and melt over medium heat. Add the onion and cook for 4 to 5 minutes, or until soft. While the onion is cooking, add the beef stock to the skillet. Deglaze the pan by scraping the bits from the bottom. If you are not using mushrooms, you can add the garlic to the onions and cook for 1 additional minute. If using mushrooms, wait until the mushrooms are sautéing to add the garlic. Place the meat in the pot along with the onion soup mix, soy sauce, Worcestershire sauce and water. Whisk to combine. Cover partially, bring to a boil and then reduce to low.

For you mushroom folks, here's where we chart our own path. Add 1 tablespoon (14 g) of butter and 1 tablespoon (15 ml) of vegetable oil to a clean pan and place over medium heat. Once the butter has melted, place the mushrooms in the pan. Cook for 4 to 5 minutes or until the mushrooms begin to soften, stirring occasionally. After about 4 minutes, season with salt and pepper and cook for 2 minutes. Add the remaining butter and the garlic and turn off the heat. Stir to combine and then add to the meat. Stir the meat and mushrooms to combine and simmer over medium-low heat for 1 hour, or until the meat is tender. Serve over nice fluffy rice.

CHICKEN AND GARLIC BUTTER DUMPLINGS

I have two words as to why I love this dish: soup, biscuits. That's right, I said it. These dumplings ain't nothin' but some soup biscuits and I love it. Alright, so maybe it's more than just the soup biscuits. It's also the delicious braised chicken that gets chopped up, delicious skin and all, into the delicious broth. Then, just when you thought it couldn't get any more deliciouser, a healthy dose of heavy cream is added to give this savory delight a silky-smooth finish. Yeah, this is one delish dish. Enjoy.

For the Chicken

1 whole chicken, quartered

Kosher salt, for seasoning

Freshly ground black pepper, for seasoning

Garlic powder, for seasoning

Paprika, for seasoning

2 tbsp (28 g) unsalted butter

2 tbsp (30 ml) extra-virgin olive oil

11 cups (2.5 L) water, divided

1 large onion, finely chopped

3 medium carrots, peeled and diced

2 celery ribs, chopped

4 cloves garlic, minced

1 tsp chopped fresh thyme

5 fresh sage leaves, chopped

2 bay leaves

1 cup (240 ml) heavy cream

Freshly chopped parsley, for serving

For the Garlic Butter Dumplings

1 clove garlic, minced

3 tbsp (42 g) butter

1½ cups (188 g) all-purpose flour

1 tbsp (14 g) baking powder

½ tsp kosher salt

1 large egg

⅔ cup (160 ml) buttermilk

To make the chicken, season both sides of the chicken with the salt, pepper, garlic powder and paprika. Place the butter and olive oil in a cast-iron skillet and melt over medium heat. Place the chicken skin side down in the skillet and cook for 5 minutes, or until browned. Turn the chicken over and cook for 3 minutes, or until that side begins to brown. Remove from the heat and place the chicken in a large stockpot with 10 cups (2.4 L) of the water, leaving the butter and oil in the skillet. Bring the pot to a boil, and then skim the foam off the top. Reduce the heat and simmer, partially covered, for 30 minutes. Remove the breasts and cook the rest of the chicken for 30 minutes.

Heat the skillet with the chicken drippings over medium heat. Add the onion, carrots and celery, season with salt and pepper and cook for 5 minutes, or until soft. Add the garlic, thyme, sage and bay leaves and cook for 1 minute. Add the contents of the skillet to the pot with the chicken. Add the remaining water to the skillet and scrape the bottom of the pan. Add any bits from the bottom of the pan to the pot and simmer for 10 minutes, or until the thickest parts of the chicken are easily pierced with a fork. Remove the chicken, shred it and set it aside.

For the dumplings, while the soup is still simmering, add the garlic to the butter and microwave for 30 seconds. In a large bowl, combine the flour, baking powder and salt. Add the egg, buttermilk and melted garlic butter to the dry ingredients and stir until combined.

Add the shredded chicken and heavy cream to the pot, mix and return to a simmer. Drop spoonfuls of dumpling mix into the pot, cover and cook over low heat for 5 minutes, or until the dumplings are cooked through. Remove the bay leaves. Serve warm, topped with fresh parsley.

SHORT RIB GRILLADES

This might be my favorite dish to put some meat on your bones. The fall-off-the-bone-tender short ribs seem to melt into the bed of delicious cheese grits. A well-deserved splash of the short rib au jus and . . . chef's kiss.

This dish is a prime example of why, oddly enough, I don't watch many cooking shows. After several attempts, I finally perfected my recipe for short ribs. I just needed a good side to accompany them. Mashed potatoes? Nah. Rice? No thanks. Cheese grits? Oh, now that's perfect. I'm a doggone genius! I whipped up a batch of short ribs, piled them high atop some delicious Cheddary grits, posted a beautiful picture and just sat back and waited for the likes to roll in.

"Looks great!" – TY!
"Ooh, yum!" – Thanks!
"Heart eyes emoji." – Smiley face
"Heart eyes emoji." – Smiley face
"Ooh, I love grillades!" – Um, thanks?

At that point, I had never even heard of grillades, so a quick Google search was in order. I searched it up as the kids say, and yup, that was pretty much it. Meat on grits. Usually a different cut of meat . . . but same concept. Oh, well . . . so apparently I didn't invent this dish, but it's still one of my favorites.

For the Short Ribs

3 lbs (1.5 kg) English-style beef short ribs

1 tsp kosher salt, plus extra for seasoning

1 tsp freshly ground pepper, plus extra for seasoning

¼ cup (31 g) all-purpose flour

1 medium onion, chopped

2 (12-oz [355-ml]) bottles Guinness Stout

2 beef bouillon cubes

1 tbsp (15 g) tomato paste

1 tbsp (9 g) minced garlic

10 sprigs fresh thyme

¼ tsp dried oregano

3 bay leaves

1 (14.5-oz [411-g]) can stewed tomatoes

2 tbsp (8 g) chopped fresh parsley

Preheat the oven to 325°F (165°C).

To make the ribs, heat a cast-iron skillet over medium-high heat. Season the short ribs generously on all sides with salt and pepper and coat them with the flour. Placing the short ribs fat side down, cook for 2 to 3 minutes, or until the fat has begun to render. Turn the short ribs to brown on the side and cook for 2 minutes. Continue turning until brown on all sides, 8 to 10 minutes total. When done, turn the heat to low and remove the short ribs from the skillet, leaving the rendered fat in the pan.

Pour the fat into a Dutch oven and place over medium heat. Add the onion and cook for 3 to 4 minutes, or until it begins to soften. While the onion is cooking, add the Guinness to the skillet to deglaze the pan. Scrape the bottom of the skillet with a wooden spoon to remove the bits stuck to the bottom. Add the beef bouillon to the Guinness and whisk to dissolve. Once the bouillon has dissolved, whisk in the tomato paste and cut off the heat. Once the onion begins to soften, add the garlic, thyme, oregano, bay leaves, salt and pepper and cook for 1 minute, or until the onion becomes aromatic.

Place the short ribs in the Dutch oven along with the stewed tomatoes, parsley and bouillon mixture from the skillet. Add enough water to the pot so the short ribs are completely submerged. Place the lid on top of the Dutch oven and place in the preheated oven for 2½ hours, or until the ribs are tender. To check if they're done, use a pair of tongs to grab one of the short ribs by the bone and remove it from the pot. The bone should easily slide out from the meat, leaving the meat in the pot.

For the Grits

1½ cups (360 ml) water

1 tsp salt

½ cup (120 ml) beef stock

1 cup (156 g) yellow stone-ground grits (I prefer Geechie Boy Mill or Anson Mills)

2 cups (450 g) shredded sharp Cheddar cheese

3 tbsp (42 g) unsalted butter

Remove the Dutch oven from the oven and place it on the stovetop. Using a pair of tongs, carefully remove the short ribs from the pot and set them on a cutting board to cool for 10 minutes. Leave the au jus in the Dutch oven as you'll be bathing the meats in that later. While the meat is cooling, prepare the grits.

To make the grits, in a medium-size pot, add the water, salt and beef stock to a medium-size pot and bring to a boil. Whisk in the grits and turn the heat down to low. Simmer, partially covered, for 10 minutes, or until most of the water has been absorbed. Add the cheese and butter to the grits and stir to combine. Cook for 5 minutes, or until the grits begin to thicken, and then turn off the heat.

Now it's time to trim the short ribs. Remove the bone and cut the meat away from the cartilage. I like to remove all the bones, chop up the meat and then place the meat in a pot with some of the au jus from the Dutch oven. You can also trim the meat and leave it intact. Either way. Spoon some of the grits onto a plate or into a bowl, place some meat on top and spoon some of the au jus (remove the bay leaves) on top of the delicious and succulent meats. Enjoy.

SOUL SATISFYING SPAGHETTI

YIELD: 4 SERVINGS

Two words why I love this spaghetti: cheesy, meat. Cheese is added during the last part of the browning of the meat for just long enough to let it caramelize and become one with the meat. It's just one way of adding a level of flavor to this dish. Looking back, spaghetti might have been my first foray into real from-scratch cooking. My mother's spaghetti was one of my favorite meals growing up—it was a good jar of sauce with lots of fresh items thrown in and it was delicious. However, it was not from scratch. It wasn't until a friend tried my amped-up jar sauce that I was so proud of and questioned why I didn't make the sauce from scratch. First of all, I was crestfallen. This semi-homemade sauce that was good enough for my momma had now been considered less than, and it was up to me to avenge this slight. And so began my quest to try and make all of my recipes, including my tomato sauce, from scratch. Now I grow my own tomatoes and herbs and make my own pasta (though not for this dish). Momma might be proud. Then again, she might just say, "Boy, go hand me that jar of Ragú off the top shelf and stop all that foolishness."

3 tbsp (45 ml) extra-virgin olive oil, divided

4 shallots, diced

5 cloves garlic, minced

2 bay leaves

2 tsp (12 g) kosher salt, divided, plus more to taste

1 tsp freshly ground black pepper, divided, plus more to taste

¼ tsp crushed red pepper flakes

6 cups (1 kg) chopped fresh tomatoes

1¼ tsp (1 g) chopped fresh thyme

1 lb (454 g) ground beef

½ tsp garlic powder

1 tsp dried oregano

1 cup (100 g) grated Pecorino Romano cheese

3 cups (720 ml) beef stock

2 tbsp (30 g) tomato paste

1 tsp sugar

1 tsp soy sauce

1 (10-oz [283-g]) box spaghetti

Heat 2 tablespoons (30 ml) of the olive oil in a large pot over medium heat. Add the shallots and cook for 4 to 5 minutes, or until soft. Add the garlic and bay leaves and season with ½ teaspoon of salt, ½ teaspoon of pepper and the crushed red pepper flakes and cook for 2 minutes. While that cooks, add the tomatoes to a blender, in batches if necessary, and puree for 30 seconds, or until smooth. Add the tomatoes and thyme to the pot and simmer over low heat.

While the tomatoes simmer, place a large skillet over medium-high heat, and add the remaining olive oil and the meat. Season with the garlic powder, oregano, ½ teaspoon of salt and the remaining pepper. Stirring occasionally, cook for 5 to 7 minutes, or until browned. Drain the meat in a colander, and then return the meat to the hot skillet. Add the Pecorino and toss like a boss to combine. Cook for 1 minute, and then add the meat to the pot with the tomatoes.

Remove the skillet from the heat, and add the beef stock and whisk in the tomato paste. Deglaze the pan by scraping the bottom with a wooden spoon, and then add the contents to the pot. Bring to a boil, and then reduce the heat to low and simmer for 10 minutes, partially covered. Remove the lid and add the remaining salt, pepper (as desired), the sugar and soy sauce. Stir to combine. Simmer for 1 hour, stirring occasionally.

In a large saucepan of salted boiling water, cook the spaghetti until al dente. Drain the pasta, reserving 3 tablespoons (45 ml) of pasta liquid. Add the pasta and pasta liquid to the sauce and stir to combine. Remove the bay leaves. Congrats! Your spaghetti is now better than my mom's.

SOUTHERN FRIED CORNISH HENS

There are three things I focus on in all of my recipes: flavor, texture and ratio . . . with the last two being highly underrated IMHHO. Everyone loves chicken wings (except for chickens, I guess). Why? Because they have an amazing balance of deliciously crispy skin to meat. Each bite, a little bit of skin, a little bit of meat. While there might be more skin or more meat on other parts of the bird, that beautiful harmony just isn't there. This is probably why Buffalo chicken backs never became a party favorite. And that's where these perfect little birdies come into play. The buttermilk brine in this recipe will help tenderize the chicken and create crispy, flavorful skin, but it's using the little bitty hens, which helps out with that delectable skin-to-meat balance. With one mouthwatering bite, you get a white and dark meat flavor explosion. It's almost as if you've floated into some chicken wing nirvana. Be careful, though. A few more tasty bites and this transcendental fried bird trip is over.

For the Chicken and Brine

1 qt (960 ml) buttermilk

1 tbsp (18 g) kosher salt

2 tsp (4 g) freshly ground black pepper

2 tsp (5 g) garlic powder

2 tsp (3 g) poultry seasoning

2 tbsp (14 g) paprika

3 tbsp (45 ml) hot sauce

4 Cornish hens, split in half lengthwise

Peanut oil, as needed

For the Dry Ingredients

4 cups (500 g) all-purpose flour

5 tbsp (90 g) salt

4 tbsp (26 g) freshly ground black pepper

1 tbsp (7 g) paprika

1 tbsp (8 g) garlic powder

1 tsp cayenne pepper

1 tsp poultry seasoning

For the chicken and brine, in a large bowl whisk together the buttermilk, salt, pepper, garlic powder, poultry seasoning, paprika and hot sauce. Place the Cornish hens in one or more resealable plastic bags and pour in the brine. Seal the bag(s), and then give a little rub down each bag to make sure the brine is distributed evenly. Place the birds in the fridge for anywhere between 3 to 24 hours to let them soak up all that fantastical buttermilk brine.

Preheat the peanut oil in a deep pan using a deep-fry thermometer or deep fryer set to 325°F (165°C).

For the dry ingredients, in a large casserole dish, combine the flour, salt, pepper, paprika, garlic powder, cayenne, and poultry seasoning.

Using tongs, and working with one piece at a time, remove the birds from the brine and place in the seasoned flour. Coat both sides with the flour, making sure to push the chicken into the flour to thoroughly coat. Place two pieces of the hen in the oil and fry, rotating the pieces every 3 to 4 minutes. Once the internal temperature reaches 165°F (75°C), 12 to 15 minutes, remove the cute little birdies from the oil and let them drain for 5 minutes. Serve and enjoy.

CHICKEN FRIED STEAK WITH GRAVY

I have to admit that when I first saw this dish on a menu, my body went through a wide range of emotions. At first there was confusion. Well, is it chicken or is it steak? Then there was anger. Wait, someone took a perfectly good ribeye and fried it like some chicken? Then there was joy. Oh, somebody took one of those cube steaks my momma used to make and battered it, fried it up golden brown and bathed it in gravy. Now that's something I can get down with.

For the Chicken Fried Steak

2 large eggs

1½ cups (360 ml) milk

1½ cups (188 g) all-purpose flour

2 tsp (12 g) salt

2½ tsp (5 g) black pepper

¼ tsp cayenne pepper

½ tsp garlic powder

½ tsp onion powder

3 lbs (1.5 kg) cube steak

2 cups (480 ml) canola or vegetable oil

For the Gravy

¼ cup (57 g) unsalted butter

4 tbsp (31 g) all-purpose flour

1½ cups (360 ml) milk

Salt, to taste

Freshly ground black pepper, to taste

In a small dish, beat the eggs and then add the milk. In a second shallow dish, mix together the flour, salt, pepper, cayenne, garlic powder and onion powder. Place the steak in the flour mixture and turn to coat. Place the meat into the milk and egg mixture, turn to coat, and then place it back in the flour and turn to coat. Place the breaded meat on a clean plate, and then repeat with the remaining meat.

Add the oil to a large skillet. Heat over medium heat until the oil reaches 350°F (180°C). Cook the meat, two to three pieces at a time, until the edges start to look golden brown, about 2 minutes on each side. Once finished, remove the meat and place on a wire rack or paper towel–lined plate to drain. Repeat until all the meat is cooked.

To make the gravy, in a small saucepan, melt the butter over medium heat. Add the flour and whisk to combine. Slowly add the milk to the pan and whisk to incorporate. Keep whisking until smooth. If the gravy appears too thick add a bit more milk, 1 tablespoon (15 ml) at a time until it thins out. Season with salt and pepper to taste. Once the gravy is the desired consistency, remove from the heat. Serve the steak with the delicious gravy spooned atop.

SEA ISLAND RED PEAS AND CAROLINA GOLD RICE HOPPIN' JOHN

This is, without a doubt, the crown jewel of my "low-country awakening." I wasn't really exposed to Creole Southern food and culture until I moved to the Gulf Coast. I was enamored with gumbo, shrimp creole and crawfish boil recipes that my friends and their families had passed down for generations. It wasn't until I started researching for this book that I was reminded of my own family's rich heritage in the low-country.

Growing up, my mother, a native of Savannah, Georgia, always talked about my Gullah cousins in the Sea Islands. When I was about ten years old, we had a family reunion in South Carolina, and I got the chance to meet some of them on Daufuskie Island. Their dialect fascinated me, and I was determined to learn more about them and other members of my family. Of course, I was ten, and there was no Internet, so by the time we got back to the hotel, I'd forgotten all about it. This, however, is my ever-so-meager attempt to pay homage to my ancestors of that region and the people of the low-country.

In researching for this recipe, two things stuck out to me. One, don't use black-eyed peas (although no judgment if you decide to do so), and two, there is a lot of technique involved in making this dish. The rice is not supposed to be cooked separately, but rather, with the peas. Traditionally cooked in a large pot over a fire, the final step in the cooking process was to let the rice "steam" or to remove it from the fire and set in the ashes. This was done all while resisting a peek in the pot as to not disturb the rice. The result? Each grain would be separate and distinct, yet infused with all the flavors of the pot. I absolutely loved this dish because I'm a process nerd and loved trying to perfect it, and the mouth feel and texture are so different from the red beans recipe, but equally as delicious.

1 smoked turkey leg or ham hock

1 medium onion, ½ sliced, ½ diced, divided

2 bay leaves, divided

4 cloves garlic, mashed, plus 1 minced, divided

5½ qt (5.5 L) water, divided

1 lb (454 g) Sea Island red peas or cowpeas

2 tbsp (28 g) unsalted butter

1 celery rib, diced

1½ tsp (9 g) salt

½ tsp pepper

¼ tsp garlic powder

¼ tsp cayenne pepper

1 cup (200 g) Carolina Gold rice or other long-grain rice, rinsed

Place the turkey leg, sliced onion, 1 bay leaf, the mashed garlic cloves and 5 quarts (5 L) of the water in a large stockpot and bring to a boil. Reduce the heat to medium-low and cook, partially covered, for 2 hours, adding water if the meat becomes exposed. Add the peas and stir to combine. Bring to a boil, and then reduce to a simmer for 1 hour.

While the peas cook, melt the butter in a pan over medium heat. Add the diced onion and cook for 2 minutes, or until it begins to soften. Add the celery and season with the salt, pepper, garlic powder and cayenne. Cook for 2 minutes, and then add the minced garlic and remaining bay leaf. Cook for 1 minute, or until the garlic becomes fragrant. Remove from the heat and add to the pot with the peas. Add the remaining water and bring to a boil. Then, reduce to a simmer and place the lid on. Cook for 30 minutes.

Add the rice to the pot, stirring to make sure all the rice is covered. Place the lid back on and simmer over low heat for 25 minutes, or until the rice is tender. Turn off the heat and let it sit in the pot for 10 minutes. Remove the bay leaves, fluff with a fork and enjoy.

SMOTHERED TURKEY WINGS

There's just something magical about a good smothered dish. The rustic, savory flavors seem to get into every morsel of the tender, delicious bird. Add in some cream at just the right time and it becomes silky smooth and delicious. Now that I think about it, I believe Article 5, Section 13, Paragraph 2 of the Soul Food Rules, Regulations, Bylaws and Thangs reads as follows: No one shall, in the course of creating a book including, claiming or purporting to claim recipes rooted in, inspired by or kinda sorta looking like soul food in name, sight or taste, create said book without the inclusion of at least one dish that shall be smothered. Here is said dish.

For the Meat

2 tsp (12 g) salt

2 tsp (4 g) freshly ground black pepper

1 tsp onion powder

¼ tsp poultry seasoning

1 tsp garlic powder

1½ tsp (1 g) smoked paprika

2 lbs (907 g) turkey wings or legs

1½ cups (188 g) all-purpose flour

½ cup (120 ml) vegetable oil

1 medium-size onion, chopped

1 celery rib, diced

2 tsp (5 g) minced garlic

For the Gravy

3 tbsp (42 g) butter

3 tbsp (24 g) flour, reserved from the freezer bag

2 cups (480 ml) chicken stock

1 cup (120 ml) heavy cream

1 bay leaf

Preheat the oven to 325°F (165°C).

To make the meat, in a bowl, combine the salt, pepper, onion powder, poultry seasoning, garlic powder and smoked paprika and season the turkey with it. Place the turkey and flour into a large freezer bag and close. Shake the bag until all of the turkey is coated with the flour. Reserve 3 tablespoons (24 g) of the flour for the gravy.

Place the oil in a large cast-iron skillet or pan over medium heat. Once the oil is hot, add the turkey. Brown the turkey on all sides, and then remove from the pan and place in a Dutch oven or large baking dish. Place the onion and celery in the oil from the turkey and cook for 3 to 4 minutes, or until just soft. Add the garlic and cook for 1 minute.

Place the onion, celery and garlic in the Dutch oven with the turkey, cover and place in the oven. Bake for 2½ hours. The turkey should be tender and beginning to fall off the bone.

While the turkey is cooking, prepare the gravy. Pour off the remaining oil in the skillet, and add the butter over medium heat. Once the butter has melted, whisk in the 3 tablespoons (24 g) of flour from the freezer bag. Slowly whisk in the stock and cream to combine. Add the bay leaf and simmer over low for 2 to 3 minutes, or until the gravy has thickened a bit. Remove the turkey from the oven and pour the gravy on top. Remove the bay leaf. Place the cover back on top of the Dutch oven and return to the oven. Cook for 1 hour. This dish is best served with mashed potatoes or rice.

TOMATO PIE

What comes to mind when you hear the words tomato pie? Is it a pizza? Is it a quiche? Is it, God forbid, some kind of dessert using tomatoes? Fortunately, tomato pie is actually a delicious savory pie that takes advantage of the bounty of fresh tomatoes available during tomato season. If you've never had it before, this recipe might make you wish that you'd discovered it sooner. Especially if you've got cheese in the piecrust to get that thing poppin'.

For the Dough

2½ cups (313 g) all-purpose flour

½ cup (125 g) microplaned Parmesan cheese

¾ tsp kosher salt

1 cup (226 g) very cold unsalted butter, cut into ½" (1.3-cm) cubes

4–8 tbsp (60–120 ml) ice water

For the Filling

3½ lbs (1.75 kg) tomatoes (about 12), cut into ½" (1.3-cm)-thick slices, plus 1 extra, sliced, for serving

2 tbsp (30 ml) olive oil

2 tsp (10 ml) balsamic vinegar

¼ tsp salt, plus more for seasoning

½ tsp freshly ground black pepper

½ tsp sugar

1 large yellow onion, thinly sliced with the grain

3 cloves garlic, thinly sliced

1 tsp fresh thyme

1 tbsp (15 ml) melted butter

2 tbsp (30 ml) extra-virgin olive oil

½ cup (120 ml) mayonnaise

⅓ cup (33 g) grated Parmigiano-Reggiano cheese

⅓ cup (149 g) smoked gouda cheese

⅓ cup (37 g) shredded sharp Cheddar cheese

⅓ cup (16 g) chopped whole basil leaves

To make the dough, pulse the flour, cheese and salt in a food processor until combined. Add the butter and pulse until the mixture resembles a coarse meal. Drizzle in the water until the dough just begins to come together. Remove from the processor and lightly knead the dough into a ball. Flatten it into a disk and wrap tightly in plastic wrap. Chill in the fridge for at least 1 hour.

Preheat the oven to 400°F (200°C).

With a floured rolling pin, roll the chilled dough on a floured surface into a 15-inch (38-cm) round. Transfer it to a deep, 9-inch (23-cm) pie pan. Trim the edges, leaving a 1-inch (2.5-cm) overhang. Fold the dough over the sides of the dish and press to seal. Using your thumb and forefinger, crimp the rim of the crust. Pop it in the fridge until you're ready to use it.

Before baking, line the piecrust with parchment paper and fill with rice or dried beans as weights, and then bake for 15 minutes. Remove the parchment paper and weights and bake for 5 minutes. Set aside to cool while you prepare the filling. Do not turn off the oven.

To make the filling, arrange the tomato slices in a single layer on a lightly greased wire rack set on a large baking sheet. Drizzle with olive oil and balsamic vinegar and cook for 30 minutes. Remove from the oven and set aside to cool for 20 minutes. Place the tomatoes in a large bowl with the salt, pepper, sugar, onion, garlic, thyme, melted butter and olive oil and mix to combine. In a separate bowl, mix together the mayo, Parmigiano-Reggiano and gouda. Meanwhile, cut the extra tomato into ½-inch (1.3-cm)-thick slices. Sprinkle with salt, cover with paper towels and set aside.

To make the pie, spread the Cheddar cheese onto the piecrust. Top the Cheddar cheese with the tomato mixture, and then top the tomatoes with the basil. Carefully spread the mayo mixture on top of the basil. Place the extra tomato slices on top, and place aluminum foil on the edges of the piecrust to keep it from burning. Bake for 40 to 45 minutes. Transfer to a wire rack and let stand for 1 hour to cool. Enjoy your mater pie.

PECAN SMOKED CHICKEN WITH ALABAMMY WHITE SAUCE

This being my first cookbook (and hopefully not my last . . . y'all don't bootleg my book to make sure it's hittin' on all the charts), I had to include at least one BBQ recipe to honor my father. My pops was the neighborhood grill guy. Whenever that BBQ smoke was billowing from our backyard, all my neighborhood friends would stop by to grab a burger or a bite of whatever he might have on the grill that day. I can remember at a fairly young age asking him what the secret was to his barbecue. His response was, "The flavor is all in the smoke. Everything else is just complementary." That little tidbit stuck with me to this day and is hopefully well represented in this recipe.

4 cups (360 g) pecan chips, for smoking, or as needed

1 tsp salt

1 tsp paprika

1 tsp garlic powder

1½ tsp (3 g) black pepper

¼ tsp cayenne pepper

1 whole chicken, cut up

Alabama White Sauce (page 135), for drizzling

Place the pecan wood chips in a large bowl. Cover the chips with water and set aside as you prepare the chicken.

In a medium-size bowl, mix together the salt, paprika, garlic powder, pepper and cayenne. Sprinkle the seasoning over the chicken, cover with plastic wrap and place in the refrigerator for 30 minutes. This is a good time to prepare the Alabama White Sauce.

If using a gas grill, place the drained wood chips in the smoking tray of the grill. If your grill does not have a smoking tray, you can make a packet out of aluminum foil by placing the drained chips in aluminum foil, wrapping it up and punching a few holes in the top. Place the smoking tray or foil packet directly on the cooking grate about 10 minutes before cooking. If using a charcoal grill, place the drained wood chips directly on the hot coals about 5 minutes before cooking.

After making sure the grill is hot, place the chicken on the grill over medium-high heat. The cover of the grill should be closed with the vents slightly ajar to help keep the smoke circulating around the meat. Check the chicken after about 5 minutes for any hot spots or flare-ups. After 15 minutes, flip the chicken over and cook for 15 minutes, checking every 5 minutes or so to make sure there are no flare-ups. Cook until a meat or instant-read thermometer reads 160°F (70°C) at the thickest part of the chicken. Remove the chicken and allow it to rest for 5 minutes. The chicken will continue to cook once coming off the grill and should have a final temperature of 165°F (75°C). Drizzle the chicken with that delicious Alabama White Sauce. It's tangy, sweet and delicious, so no need to bathe your bird in it.

SKRIMPS AND SUCH

I've always had an affinity for seafood. Even though I grew up in the Midwest, my mother's upbringing on the Georgia coast had a heavy influence on our diet. While corned beef and cabbage may have been a staple for some, we were more likely to have deviled crab, red rice with shrimp or she-crab soup. Growing up, I always assumed that as an adult, I'd be living somewhere off the coast with incredible access to all types of seafood. Unfortunately, that has not come to fruition . . . yet. However, I'm still making magic with good seafood whenever I can find it. One of my favorite things to make, seafood or not, is gumbo. A delicious homemade stock along with a slow, deep, dark roux gives my Roux-Let-the-Dogs-Out Shrimp and Sausage Gumbo (page 50) a rich flavor. Another one of my favorites in this chapter is the New Orleans BBQ Shrimp recipe (page 58). It's a dish that I believe is unique to New Orleans, and I really hope to introduce more people to its unparalleled flavor.

ROUX-LET-THE-DOGS-OUT SHRIMP AND SAUSAGE GUMBO

YIELD: 6 SERVINGS

Anytime someone asks what my favorite thing is to make, I always answer, hands down: gumbo. I love the whole process of cooking, and making gumbo from scratch is a perfect example of this. Taking scraps of shrimp shells, veggies and herbs and letting them simmer to create a rich stock. Then slowly cooking the oil and flour to create a deep, dark roux. I love the sausage and shrimp combination in this gumbo, but you can really toss whatever you like into it.

1 lb (454 g) andouille or smoked sausage, sliced

¾ cup (180 ml) vegetable oil

1 cup (125 g) all-purpose flour

2 cups (320 g) chopped onion

1½ cups (137 g) chopped green bell pepper

3 celery ribs, chopped

5 cloves garlic, minced

2 bay leaves

¼ tsp fresh thyme

1 tbsp (18 g) kosher salt, plus more to taste

½ tsp garlic powder

¼ tsp cayenne pepper

2 qt (2 L) shrimp stock

3 blue crabs, cleaned and dressed

½ tsp Worcestershire sauce

2 lbs (907 g) medium fresh shrimp, peeled and deveined

¼ cup (15 g) chopped fresh parsley

Rice, for serving

¼ cup (12 g) chopped green onion, for serving

Place the sausage in a large skillet over medium-high heat and cook, stirring occasionally, for 5 minutes, or until browned. Remove the sausage from the heat and drain. Set aside.

Place the vegetable oil in the skillet and heat over medium heat. Whisk in the flour and stir together to form a roux. Cook over medium-low heat, stirring continuously. If you prefer a lighter roux, cook for approximately 10 to 15 minutes. If you like your roux darker, continue cooking up to an additional 30 minutes (45 minutes total), depending on how dark you like your roux. Be careful not to burn it. If it starts smoking too much, reduce the heat to low.

Once the roux is to your liking, add the onion, bell pepper and celery and cook for 5 minutes, or until the veggies begin to soften, stirring often. Add the garlic, bay leaves, thyme, salt, garlic powder and cayenne and cook for 2 minutes. Transfer the roux and veggies to a large stockpot along with the shrimp stock and bring the mixture to a boil. Add the sausage, crabs and Worcestershire sauce and reduce the heat to medium. Simmer for 1 hour, skimming the top and stirring occasionally.

Turn the heat off and add the shrimp. Let them sit for about 3 minutes or until they become opaque. Add the parsley. Salt to taste, remove the bay leaves and serve with rice, topped with green onion.

SALMON CROQUETTES

This is another one of my mother's recipes that I loved as a child. Crispy fried salmon patties with chunky bell pepper and onion to give it a fresh pop in each bite. The whole house would smell like fish for two days after she fried them, but we didn't give a hooey. As recipes evolve and grow, I've seen this dish made recently using fresh salmon; however, I'm sticking with the OG recipe here. Salmon croquettes became popular both because, at the time, canned salmon was less expensive than fresh, and access to fresh fish was limited in some parts of the country. If you're ready for a tasty salmon treat, crack a window, light a candle and get to fryin'.

2 (14.75-oz [418-g]) cans red salmon (as my mother would say, "Use the red, not that pink stuff. It has more flavor, baby.")

2 eggs, beaten

½ cup (75 g) chopped green bell pepper

½ cup (80 g) diced onion

1 tsp paprika

1 tsp garlic powder

2 tsp (8 g) salt

¼ tsp celery seed

2 tbsp (16 g) all-purpose flour

2 cups (480 ml) vegetable oil

Secret Tartar Sauce (page 143), for serving

Drain the salmon and place it in a large bowl. I pick out the large bones (the spine) and leave the small ones (mmm . . . bone flavor). The little ones are very soft, and you won't notice them when the salmon is mixed together. I also leave the skin on (mmm . . . skin flavor) 'cause I'm all about that flavor life. You can pick out all the bones and skin if you like, depending on how picky (see what I did there) you are. A fancy-pants skinless variety of salmon is also available if you can find it.

Add the eggs, bell pepper, onion, paprika, garlic powder, salt and celery seed and give it a light mix. Sprinkle in the flour and lightly mix again. The mixture should be, dare I say. . . moist, and not too dry. Cover and place in the fridge for 1 hour.

Heat the oil over medium-high heat in a skillet. Add a bit of oil to your hands (not from the hot pan of course), and form the salmon mixture into small patties, about 3 tablespoons (45 g) each, or until you have eight patties. Carefully drop them into the oil immediately after forming, being cautious not to fry your fingertips. Cook for 3 minutes, flip and cook for 3 minutes on the other side. Remove with a slotted spoon and place on a wire rack or paper towel–lined plate. Serve with the Secret Tartar Sauce and enjoy. (Confession: As a kid, I used to eat these with ketchup, and to this day, I still must eat at least one out of the bunch with ketchup for old time's sake. #boneappleteeth)

SHRIMP AND GRITS

As you can see, grits have made yet another appearance in this book. As a mainstay in soul food and Southern cooking, I think at this point we can place them among okra and sweet potatoes as one of the heavyweights of soul food ingredients. While eaten in many different ways at different times throughout history across the globe, grits hold a special place in the soul food cookbook. Once given to enslaved Africans as a cheap food source, grits could be found in varying forms on the plate of both the slave master and the enslaved. Now, with special heirloom varieties of corn being produced, grits are finding their way into elevated soul food and Southern cuisine all across the country. I love this dish because it gets a flavor injection from several different sources, creating levels and levels of flavor. It starts off with the rendered fat of the sausage. Then, the addition of shrimp shells to the chicken stock helps to create an incredibly rich and flavorful stock. Finally, the gouda added to the grits gives it a fabulously smooth little zip at the end. Bravo me . . . and you!

For the Shrimp

1½ lbs (680 g) fresh shrimp, shells on

1 qt (960 ml) plus 2 cups (480 ml) chicken stock, divided

2 cups (430 g) diced smoked sausage or tasso ham

1 tsp salt, divided

¼ cup (57 g) butter

¼ cup (31 g) all-purpose flour

½ small onion, diced

½ cup (75 g) diced red bell pepper

1 tsp minced garlic

1 tsp freshly squeezed lemon juice

3 green onions, chopped, plus more for garnish

For the Grits

2 cups (480 ml) water

1 tsp salt

2 cups (480 ml) chicken stock and/or shrimp stock

2 cups (312 g) stone-ground grits

2 cups (226 g) shredded gouda

1 tbsp (14 g) butter

1 cup (240 ml) heavy cream

To make the shrimp, remove the shrimp shells and tails and place the shells in a medium-size saucepan. Cover with 2 cups (480 ml) of the chicken stock and bring to a boil. Once boiling, reduce the heat to low and simmer for 5 minutes. Remove from the heat and set aside.

Place the sausage in a pan over medium-high heat and cook for 5 minutes, or until browned, turning occasionally. Remove the sausage from the pan, leaving the rendered fat in the pan, and set aside. Place the shrimp in the pan with the sausage fat and season with ½ teaspoon of the salt. Cook over medium-high heat for 1 to 2 minutes per side, or until just opaque. Remove the shrimp from the pan and set aside.

Add the butter to a clean pan over medium-low heat. Once the butter has melted, whisk in the flour and stir constantly. Cook for 6 to 7 minutes, or until the roux is the color of light peanut butter. Add the onion to the roux and cook for 3 to 4 minutes, or until soft. Add the red bell pepper and garlic and cook for 2 minutes. Season with the remaining salt. Slowly whisk in the remaining chicken stock. Add the sausage and stir to combine. Reduce the heat to low and simmer for 2 minutes. Add the shrimp, lemon juice and green onions. Cook for 1 to 2 minutes.

To make the grits, in a medium-size pot, add the water, salt and chicken and shrimp stock mixture and bring to a boil. Whisk in the grits and turn the heat to low. Simmer, partially covered, until most of the water has been absorbed, about 10 minutes. Add the gouda and butter and stir to combine. Once the gouda and butter have melted, add the heavy cream and cook for 10 minutes, or until thickened. Remove from the heat.

Spoon some of the grits onto a plate or into a bowl. Spoon some of the shrimp and sauce on top and garnish with green onion. Enjoy.

EVERYTHANG-IN-THE-POT LOW-COUNTRY SHRIMP BOIL

I can recall some of my relatives from Savannah coming to visit me while I was living in Houston. My sister and I were excited to take them to a new seafood restaurant that had just opened up that always had lines out the door. The restaurant specialized in boiled seafood that they served to you in a plastic bag. Let's call the place "Boil in a Bag." After 45 minutes of us hyping the place up while we were waiting in line, we were finally escorted to our table. My uncle took one look at the menu and said, "This ain't nothin' but a low-country shrimp boil."

Full disclosure: This recipe is probably best described as a low-country shrimp boil/Boil in a Bag hybrid. While I've heard it said that a good boil doesn't need any seasoning at the end, this is not one of those boils. We give it a nice base seasoning in the water, and then at the end it gets freaky. Garlic butter, three types of seasoning and a spice level that is all at your own discretion. That fantastic finish is what makes this low-country boil finger-licking good.

1 serrano pepper, diced (Choose your own adventure on this one. You can make it hotter by substituting habanero or more serranos.)

2 tbsp (17 g) minced garlic

½ cup (114 g) butter

2 tsp (8 g) lemon pepper seasoning

2 tsp (10 g) creole seasoning

3½ tbsp (36 g) Chesapeake Bay seasoning, divided

1–2 large roasting bags

6 qt (6 L) water

½ lemon

1 lb (454 g) smoked sausage, cut into 2" (5-cm) pieces

6 ears of corn, shucked, cut in half

14 oz (397 g) baby bella mushrooms, halved

3 lbs (1.5 kg) small new potatoes, quartered

4 lbs (1.8 kg) fresh large shrimp, shells on

3 cups (273 g) chopped broccoli

Newspaper, for serving

Place the serrano, garlic, butter, lemon pepper, creole seasoning and ½ tablespoon (4 g) of the Chesapeake Bay seasoning in one or two large roasting bags and set aside.

Fill a stockpot with the water. (If necessary, you can divide the water and ingredients between two pots.) Add the lemon and remaining Chesapeake Bay seasoning, cover and bring to a boil. Add the sausage and corn, return to a boil and cook for 10 minutes. Add the mushrooms and cook for 3 minutes. Add the potatoes, bring to a boil and cook for 6 minutes. Add the shrimp and cut off the heat. Let it sit for 2 minutes, or until the shrimp are opaque and cooked through. During that time, place the broccoli in a small colander and submerge in the pot for 1 minute. Remove the broccoli and set aside. Drain the pot and place the drained contents into the roasting bag(s) and shake to coat. Once coated, add the broccoli to the bag. Place newspaper on top of a large table and empty the contents of the bags on the newspaper. Enjoy with friends, your favorite cold beverage and sunshine on your face.

NEW ORLEANS BBQ SHRIMP

For various reasons, New Orleans has always had a special place in my heart. Every time I visit, my experience has been totally different, but it has always been incredible. There was one particular visit when I discovered New Orleans BBQ shrimp. After some day drinking and getting separated from my friends on Bourbon Street, I staggered into a restaurant to gather my thoughts and eat some lunch. Browsing the menu, I spotted it: New Orleans BBQ Shrimp. I thought to myself, "Some grilled shrimp and rice sounds pretty tasty right now . . . sold." Of course, when my food arrived, it looked nothing like the grilled shrimp I had envisioned. It was a plate full of shrimp, shell on, bathing in some kind of murky-looking sauce. Never one to shy away from a new eating adventure, I dove right in, and before I was halfway through with my plate, I was raising my hand for another serving. For that reason, this is one dish that I had to include in this book just for its sheer uniqueness. Butter, butter, some more butter and a little more butter, along with rosemary and some Worcestershire sauce, give this dish loads of flavor.

1 cup (240 ml) water

2 tbsp (30 ml) lemon juice

1 lemon, sliced

5 tbsp (75 ml) Worcestershire sauce

½ tsp black pepper

6 cloves garlic, minced

1 tsp creole seasoning

1 tbsp (2 g) chopped fresh rosemary

2 bay leaves

2 lbs (907 g) medium-to-large fresh shrimp, unpeeled

¼ cup (60 ml) white wine

1½ cups (339 g) butter, cut into 2" (5-cm) cubes

4 green onions, sliced

White rice, for serving (optional)

French bread, for sopping up goodness

In a large skillet, combine the water, lemon juice, lemon, Worcestershire sauce, black pepper, garlic and creole seasoning, and bring to a boil. Reduce the heat to medium-high and add the rosemary, bay leaves, shrimp and white wine, cooking the shrimp for about 1 minute on each side. Make sure not to cook the shrimp for too long here, otherwise they will be overcooked in the next step. After 2 minutes, reduce the heat to medium-low and stir in the butter, a couple of cubes at a time. Stir constantly, adding more butter once the previous butter has melted. Add the green onions. Remove the bay leaves, pour the contents in a bowl and serve with white rice, if desired, or French bread for sopping up the awesomeness.

SOFT-SHELLED CRAB BURGERS

I'm a fairly lazy person by nature. This is probably why I've never been a huge fan of blue crabs. I mean they're delicious and all, but it takes a whole lot of work to get to a little bitty ole piece of meat. Ah, but that's where soft-shell crabs come into play. These are crabs that have shed their protective shell so that they can form a new, larger one. With no shell to worry about, just eat that delicious little crabby in its entirety, crispy little shell, claws and all. It's probably my favorite seafood to eat, so I had to include it in this book. This recipe starts out with a light dredging in some seasoned flour, then a quick dip in an egg wash and then some panko for a deliciously crispy crunch. A nice lemony tartar sauce to top it off and you've got a crabtastic little sando in the palm of your hands.

For the Tartar Sauce

½ cup (120 ml) mayonnaise

Zest of 1 lemon

2 tsp (10 ml) lemon juice

1 tbsp (3 g) chopped capers

½ tsp cayenne pepper

For the Crabs

1 cup (125 g) flour

1½ tsp (9 g) salt

¼ tsp celery seed

¼ tsp cayenne pepper

½ tsp garlic powder

1 tsp black pepper

1 egg, beaten

⅔ cup (160 ml) milk

2 tsp (10 ml) hot sauce

2 cups (112 g) panko

2 cups (480 ml) vegetable or canola oil

4 cleaned soft-shell blue crabs (see Note)

For Serving

Butter

4 brioche slider buns

1 small red onion, thinly sliced

Red leaf lettuce

To make the tartar sauce, in a small bowl, place the mayo, zest, lemon juice, capers and cayenne and mix to combine. Cover and place in the refrigerator until ready to use.

To make the crabs, in a shallow dish, mix together the flour, salt, celery seed, cayenne, garlic powder and black pepper. In another shallow dish, mix together the egg, milk and hot sauce. Place the panko breadcrumbs in a third dish.

Dredge each crab in the flour to coat completely. Then, dip both sides in the milk mixture, and from there, dip it in the panko breading. Don't be shy about pressing it into the breading so that it sticks; however, the panko won't be perfectly coated. It's there mainly to add crunch and supplement the flour coating.

Add the oil to a skillet and heat to medium. The panko breading will burn if the heat is too high, so be sure to watch it. Carefully place the crabs in the oil—don't overcrowd them! Cook for 6 minutes, turning halfway with a pair of tongs. Remove the crabs from the oil and place on a wire rack or paper towel–lined plate.

To serve, butter the buns and toast them slightly. You can do this on top of the stove or in the oven, whatever your preference. Place one crab on the bottom bun and top with the tartar sauce. Place a few slices of red onion and then a leaf of lettuce on top of that.

NOTE: Make sure to have your fishmonger clean the crabs for you so you're not eating the inedible parts like the gills and apron.

PANFRIED SKRIMPS

Of course, with a nickname like Scotty Gump you had to expect another shrimp recipe was just around the bend. The trick to tasty fried shrimp is a well-seasoned dredging or batter and a quick fry in hot oil. Shrimp cook up quickly, so hot oil ensures they fry up light and crispy and not oily. A quick pre-fry bath in evaporated milk and hot sauce gives them an ever-so-subtle sweet-and-spicy undertone that really helps put this classic fried shrimp recipe over the top.

1 lb (454 g) peeled and deveined shrimp

1 (12-oz [355-ml]) can evaporated milk

1 egg, beaten

2 tsp (10 ml) hot sauce

1 cup (125 g) all-purpose flour

1 cup (122 g) cornmeal

1 tsp salt

½ tsp garlic powder

½ tsp paprika

1 tsp black pepper

3 cups (720 ml) vegetable oil

Tartar sauce or cocktail sauce, for serving

Place the shrimp in a large freezer bag and pour in the milk, egg and hot sauce. Close the bag and set aside for 10 minutes. In a shallow dish, mix together the flour, cornmeal, salt, garlic powder, paprika and black pepper. One at a time, remove the shrimp from the milk mixture and coat in the flour mixture, pressing down on the shrimp to make sure it is fully coated. Once coated, place the shrimp on a separate dish.

Pour the oil into a large cast-iron skillet or pan and place over medium-high heat. Working in batches, place five to six shrimp into the oil, being sure not to overcrowd the pan. Cook for 2 minutes, and then flip and cook for 2 minutes, or until golden brown. Remove the shrimp from the oil with a slotted spoon and place on a wire rack or paper towel–lined plate. Enjoy with tartar sauce (store-bought or my Secret Tartar Sauce, page 143) or cocktail sauce, whichever floats your boat.

SHRIMP AND CRAB PILAU

Pilau, perlo or purloo. This is another low-country awakening dish that is just overflowing with history and flavor. Born out of the rice lands of the Carolinas, it focuses equally on technique as well as taste. The goal of adding the rice to the pot as it cooks is to achieve light, fluffy rice with grains that are separate and distinct, not lumped together. While pilau may be made with chicken, seafood or a combination of the two, this is a seafood-only dish. Fresh tomatoes and shrimp and crab folded in at the end keep this dish fresh and remarkably light. While my technique may still be lacking a bit (the rice was a bit too sticky) the flavors of this dish are still incredible.

1½ cups (300 g) Carolina Gold or other long-grain rice

¼ cup (57 g) unsalted butter

2 cups (320 g) diced yellow onion

2 celery ribs, diced

1 cup (149 g) finely chopped red bell pepper

1 tsp salt, divided

¼ tsp pepper

¼ tsp cayenne pepper

¼ tsp celery seed

1 tsp minced garlic

¼ tsp crushed red pepper flakes

1 bay leaf

2 cups (480 ml) shrimp or seafood stock

1 tbsp (15 ml) extra-virgin olive oil

5 red tomatoes, peeled, seeded and chopped

3 tbsp (12 g) chopped fresh parsley

1 lb (454 g) medium shrimp

1 tbsp (15 ml) fresh lemon juice

1 lb (454 g) lump crab meat

Place the rice in a strainer and rinse under cool water. Shake out the strainer to remove any excess water and place the rice in a bowl to dry out.

In a Dutch oven with a tight-fitting lid, melt the butter over medium heat. Once melted, add the onion, celery, bell pepper, ¼ teaspoon of the salt, pepper, cayenne and celery seed. Cook over medium-low heat for 5 to 10 minutes, or until transparent. Add the garlic, crushed red pepper flakes and bay leaf, and cook for 1 minute, or until fragrant.

Add the stock, remaining salt and olive oil to the bowl of rice and toss to coat. Add the rice, tomatoes and parsley to the pot, stir to combine and bring to a quick boil. Lower the heat to low, cover the pot, and simmer over medium-low heat for 22 minutes without lifting the lid. Turn off the heat and remove the lid. Fluff the rice while tossing in the shrimp and lemon juice. Gently fold in the crab meat, being careful not to break it up. Place the lid back on for 5 to 7 minutes to let the warm rice cook the shrimp. Remove the bay leaf and enjoy.

THE SOUL
REMIX

This chapter, ladies and gentlemen, is where I make the magic happen. This is where I take a traditional recipe and give it a little tweak here and a little tweak there to create something special. I have to be honest with you and say that writing a soul food cookbook has been incredibly stressful. When I create new dishes, they're mine; they belong to me. Whether you love it or hate it, you can't tell me what to put in a dish that I created. Soul food is different, though. While this might be my particular version, these recipes are time-honored classics passed down through the generations. They were here long before me and will be here long after I'm gone. I can only hope that I have been a good steward of their essence during my time with them. A friend recently confided in me that he didn't really understand how cooking tried-and-true recipes could be stressful. My analogy was that it's like hearing someone butcher the national anthem. You had one job.

But here is where we get funky. Whether it be the fantastic Humdinger Red Bean Hummus (page 72), which is part red beans, part hummus and dare I say, part pâté, or the Fried Oyster Collard Green Salad (page 71), this is where we take the essence of some of the classics and turn them on their heads a bit. From Chicken and Brown Butter Sweet Potato Waffles with Maple Bourbon Sauce (page 80) to Blackened Shrimp and Fried Polenta (page 83), these dishes are going to make you say, "Who?" and "Wow!" and hopefully become some of your new favorite go-to recipes.

BLACK GARLIC SKILLET T-BONE

As the late, great Christopher "The Notorious B.I.G." Wallace once said, "A T-bone steak, cheese, eggs and Welch's grape. Conversate for a few, 'cause in a few, we gon' do what we came to do, ain't that right, Boo? True?"

So for this recipe, all it takes is a little black garlic to jazzify a dish and give it a different twist. For those unfamiliar, black garlic is garlic that has been fermented, resulting in a somewhat sweet and almost balsamic taste.

While huge $50 steakhouse steaks can be awesome, sometimes I really don't need to ingest 32 ounces (907 g) of meats in one sitting. That's when I can appreciate a nice diner-style, thin-cut T-bone. Quickly fried up on the griddle, it's perfect when I've got a hankering for steak but don't want to feel like I ate a cow.

¼ cup (57 g) butter

5 cloves black garlic (you can usually find it on Jeff Bezos' little website)

2 (1" [2.5-cm]) T-bone steaks

2 tbsp (30 ml) canola or avocado oil

Kosher salt, as needed

Freshly ground black pepper, as needed

Coarse sea salt, for serving

Place the butter in a small saucepan over medium-low heat to melt. Here's where it gets a bit tricky. Black garlic is very sticky, and the consistency is not at all like regular garlic. I usually pass it through a garlic press, but it still winds up kind of globbing together. Just pass it through the press and briskly whisk it into the melted butter. Let simmer on low for about 5 minutes as the garlic dissolves into the butter, which should turn blackish. Remove from the heat and place in a heat-safe bowl.

Preheat the oven to 450°F (230°C).

Crank up your oven exhaust to high and place a cast-iron skillet on the stove over high heat.

Brush the steaks on both sides with the oil, and then liberally apply salt and freshly ground pepper to both sides.

Place one steak at a time on the skillet and cook for 2 minutes to sear. Flip the steak, and then sear the other side for 2 minutes. Remove from the stove and place in the oven for 2 to 3 minutes. Remove from the oven and place on a cutting board to rest for 5 minutes. Plate the steak and then drizzle with the black garlic butter. Finish with a sprinkle of coarse sea salt that hopefully does not get filtered through the hairs of a man's sweaty forearm (yes you, Salt Bae) on the way down to your steak.

FRIED OYSTER COLLARD GREEN SALAD

This is hands down one of my favorite recipes in this book, mainly because it exemplifies what I try to do in my cooking. That is, take a classic dish and put just a little spin on it so that you come away with a fresh experience. And while the oysters are damn, damn tasty, you may never look at collard greens the same after this. While traditional collard greens cook for hours in a rich broth, these get their flavor from a quick roasting, which really lets the true taste of the collard greens come through. A light squeeze of lemon juice at the end brightens them up and helps offset the delicious fatty goodness of the fried oysters.

For the Collard Greens

1 bunch collard greens

Olive oil, as needed

Kosher salt, as needed

1 fresh lemon

For the Oysters

1 cup (125 g) all-purpose flour

1 cup (122 g) cornmeal

1 tsp lemon pepper seasoning

½ tsp paprika

¼ tsp onion powder

¼ tsp garlic powder

¾ tsp salt

1 egg, beaten

2 tsp (10 ml) hot sauce

½ cup (120 ml) milk

12 oysters

3 cups (720 ml) vegetable or canola oil

Creole Buttermilk Ranch (page 144)

Preheat the oven to 325°F (165°C).

To make the collard greens, remove all the stems from the collards and dry with a paper towel. Drying out the leaves ensures that they don't steam as they cook and come out crispy. Take several leaves of the same size and stack them on top of each other. I usually can do about five at a time. Once stacked, fold them over long-wise. Now, take those folded leaves and cut very thin strips across. The greens should look like shredded paper or that decorative crinkle paper that you hastily shove into a gift bag as you sit in your car trying to gussy up that last-minute birthday gift right before you walk into the birthday party.

Take those festive crinkle collards and make it rain on a large baking sheet, spreading them out evenly. Drizzle them with the olive oil and a pinch of salt and toss them to combine. Place them in the oven for 5 to 7 minutes, or until crispy. Once out of the oven, give them a light squeeze of some lemon juice and set them aside. Repeat with the remaining greens.

To make the oysters, place the flour, cornmeal, lemon pepper, paprika, onion powder, garlic powder and salt on a plate and stir to combine. Place the egg, hot sauce and milk in a dish and whisk to combine. Working in batches, lightly dredge each oyster in the flour mixture, and then dip in the milk, and then back again in the flour, making sure to coat both sides completely each time. Place on a plate and continue with the remaining oysters.

Add the oil to a medium-size cast-iron skillet or pan over medium heat. Once it's hot, one by one, gently drop the oysters into the oil, making sure not to overcrowd the pan. Cook for 6 to 7 minutes, or until golden brown, flipping halfway through. Remove from the oil and let dry on a wire rack or paper towel–lined plate. Place a handful of the collards on a salad plate. Arrange a few of the oysters on top all pretty like, and then drizzle with the Creole Buttermilk Ranch. Serve immediately.

HUMDINGER RED BEAN HUMMUS

YIELD: 4 SERVINGS

With a lot of my recipes and cooking videos, I try to recreate new dishes with the leftovers so you're not eating the exact same thing over and over. In many cases, the new recipe turns out to be just as good, if not better, than the original. This is one such recipe. A little bit of fried garlic adds depth, while the splash of lemon brightens it up. A light dusting of cayenne at the end gives your mouth one last thing to think about when it's pondering what you just ate.

¼ cup (60 ml) avocado oil

1 clove garlic, sliced

2 cups (354 g) Slow and Low Red Beans (page 26)

Juice from 1 large lemon

¼ tsp paprika

3 tbsp (45 ml) extra-virgin olive oil, plus more for drizzling

Cayenne pepper, for serving

French bread, for serving

This recipe only needs one sliced clove of garlic, but you might as well throw a couple more in there while the pot is hot, right? Place the avocado oil in a small saucepan over medium heat. Add the sliced garlic and cook for 2 to 3 minutes, flipping halfway through and breaking up the pieces that are stuck together. Remove the garlic slices from the oil and place on a paper towel to drain. Once cooled, chop up the sliced garlic, setting aside ½ teaspoon for this recipe.

Drain the beans in a colander, catching the juice in a bowl, and then scoop out the juice from the bowl and add ½ cup (120 ml) of it back in. Combine the beans, fried garlic, lemon juice, paprika and bean juice in a food processor. Process that boy for 1 minute. Add the olive oil and process for 1 minute, or until really, really, really creamy. Transfer to a shallow bowl and give it a light dusting of the cayenne pepper. Give it one last drizzle of olive oil and serve with some fresh French bread.

RUM CAKE FRENCH TOAST

I thought up this recipe one day when I really had a taste for some rum cake but was too lazy to make some rum cake . . . and honestly, this might be even better. While rum cake can be a bit dense and heavy at times, this breakfast item keeps all the light and airiness of French toast with all the delicious flavors you'd enjoy in a rum cake. A little maple syrup for the butter rum syrup makes sure it still has that breakfast vibe.

For the Butter Rum Syrup

½ cup (114 g) butter

¼ cup (60 ml) water

2 tbsp (30 g) granulated sugar

1 cup (240 ml) maple syrup

¼ cup (60 ml) rum

For the French Toast

3 eggs

1 tsp rum extract or 3 tbsp (45 ml) rum

½ tsp vanilla extract

¼ tsp salt

1 tbsp (15 g) granulated sugar

¼ tsp ground nutmeg

½ tsp ground cinnamon

1½ cups (360 ml) heavy cream

8 thick slices challah, brioche or white bread

Butter, for frying

To make the syrup, place the butter, water and sugar in a small saucepan over medium heat. Cook, stirring occasionally, for 5 minutes, or until the sugar is dissolved. Add the maple syrup and rum and cook for 2 to 3 minutes. Set aside.

Preheat the oven to 225°F (110°C).

To make the French toast, in a shallow dish, beat the eggs, rum extract, vanilla, salt, sugar, nutmeg and cinnamon. Stir in the cream. Dip one slice of bread in the egg mixture, turning to coat both sides evenly. Place a small pat of butter on a nonstick griddle or skillet over medium heat. Once melted, place a piece of bread in the butter and cook until the bread is browned, 2 to 3 minutes. Flip the bread and continue to fry for another 2 to 3 minutes, until the bread is browned on both sides. Repeat with the rest of the bread. Place the French toast in the oven to keep warm while cooking the remaining slices. Serve with the butter rum syrup.

DUCK FAT SHRIMP ETOUFFEE
WITH CRISPY ONION STRINGS

People always ask me how I come up with my recipes, and honestly, they just come to me in the most random ways. Take this one, for example. Last Thanksgiving, I was preparing my menu and decided to make green bean casserole with crispy onion strings. While continuing to make my list, and after a bit of deliberation, I came to one conclusion: I do not like green bean casserole. The only reason I was going to make it was because I really wanted the delicious crispy onion strings. And thus, this dish was born.

I love this recipe because it is a true symphony of flavors and textures. It all begins with the duck fat roux, which gives it a delicious, earthy base. The chicken stock and shrimp then each add another level of flavor to the profile. The light, fluffy rice provides a nice, soft landing spot for all of these flavors to come together, while the crispy onion strings provide a nice textural surprise not usually associated with a dish like this. It truly is one of my favorite new recipes. And to think I owe it all to my disdain for green bean casserole.

For the Etouffee

¼ cup (60 g) duck fat

¼ cup (31 g) all-purpose flour

½ cup (80 g) chopped onion

½ cup (75 g) diced green bell pepper

1 celery rib, diced

1 tbsp (9 g) minced garlic

2 tsp (12 g) salt

½ tsp black pepper

1 tsp chopped fresh thyme

½ tsp cayenne pepper

1 qt (960 ml) chicken stock

1½ lbs (680 g) fresh shrimp

For the Onion Strings

2 cups (480 ml) vegetable oil

½ tsp salt

2 tsp (4 g) freshly ground black pepper

1 cup (125 g) all-purpose flour

1 cup (240 ml) milk

½ onion, sliced thinly (about 1 cup [160 g])

Cayenne pepper, as desired

Rice, for serving

To make the etouffee, add the duck fat to a large saucepan over medium heat. Once the duck fat has melted, add the flour and stir constantly. Cook for 5 minutes. You don't want to let the roux get too dark as it will overpower the flavor of the duck fat. Add the onion, green bell pepper, celery, garlic, salt, pepper, thyme and cayenne. Cook for 4 to 5 minutes, or until the veggies have softened. Whisk in the chicken stock until fully incorporated and bring to a boil. Then, reduce to a simmer. Cook for 15 minutes, or until you reach the desired consistency. Add the shrimp and cook for 2 to 3 minutes, or until they turn opaque, and then cut off the heat.

To make the onion strings, add the oil to a small skillet over medium-high heat. Add the salt, pepper and flour to a large freezer bag and shake to combine. Pour the milk into a small dish. Working in small batches, place the onions in the milk, and then into the bag with the flour. Shake to coat the onions. Remove some of the onions, a handful at a time, shaking off the excess flour, and place in the oil. Cook for 4 to 5 minutes, or until golden brown. Remove from the oil with a slotted spoon and place on a paper towel–lined plate. Lightly dust the onion rings with cayenne. Serve the etouffee over rice with the onion strings on top.

CAJUN RED BEAN BURGERS

Another spinoff from the hit show Slow and Low Red Beans and Rice (page 26), these little Cajun burgers are packed with flavor. Instead of starting out with a boring, old can of beans they begin with some delicious, slow-cooked red beans with onion, garlic and delicious sausage. These aren't your run-of-the-mill vegetarian bean burgers. In fact, don't let one of your vegetarian friends take a bite out of these bad boys—it might just turn them to the dark side.

2½ cups (443 g) Slow and Low Red Beans (page 26)

½ cup (28 g) panko

2 tbsp (16 g) all-purpose flour

1 egg, beaten

½ tsp paprika

¼ tsp salt

¼ tsp pepper

1 cup (240 ml) olive oil

Sliced red onion, lettuce and buns, for serving

Creole Buttermilk Ranch (page 144), for serving

In a food processor, pulse the beans until coarsely chopped, and then transfer to a large mixing bowl. Add the panko, flour, egg, paprika, salt and pepper, and mix well. Divide the mixture into four equal parts. Shape into burger patties and refrigerate for 30 minutes.

Place the olive oil in a skillet over medium heat. Carefully place the bean patties in the pan two at a time. Cook for 4 minutes, and then flip. The burger should have begun to brown. Flip and cook for another 4 to 5 minutes on the other side. Remove from the heat and serve with your favorite burger condiments.

CHICKEN AND BROWN BUTTER SWEET POTATO WAFFLES WITH MAPLE BOURBON SAUCE

I'm gonna keep it 100 with you here. Chicken and waffles have had their day. Yeah, I said it. That being said, these waffles are freaking incredible. The nuttiness of the brown butter coupled with the maple bourbon sauce that I could honestly just drink by itself makes these things phenomenal. So, go ahead and make them, enjoy them and share them, because chicken and waffles' days are numbered.

For the Buttermilk Brine

1 qt (960 ml) buttermilk

1 tbsp (18 g) kosher salt

2 tsp (4 g) black pepper

2 tsp (5 g) garlic powder

2 tsp (5 g) poultry seasoning

2 tbsp (14 g) paprika

3 tbsp (45 ml) hot sauce

For the Chicken

3 lbs (1.5 kg) chicken wings

4 cups (500 g) all-purpose flour

5 tbsp (90 g) salt

4 tbsp (24 g) ground black pepper

1 tbsp (7 g) paprika

1 tbsp (8 g) garlic powder

1 tsp cayenne pepper

1 tsp poultry seasoning

1 qt (960 ml) peanut oil

For the Waffles

2 cups (250 g) all-purpose flour

2 tbsp (30 g) granulated sugar

¼ tsp nutmeg

¼ tsp cinnamon

1 tbsp (14 g) baking powder

½ tsp kosher salt

¼ tsp baking soda

2 large eggs, room temperature, beaten to blend

1 tsp vanilla extract

3 tbsp (47 g) whole-milk ricotta, room temperature

1¼ cups (300 ml) sweet potato juice (1 large sweet potato, cut into 2-inch [5-cm] cubes and fed into a juicer)

½ cup (120 ml) buttermilk

6 tbsp (90 ml) melted brown butter

1 stick butter, for brushing

Maple Bourbon Sauce (page 132)

To make the brine, in a large bowl, whisk together the buttermilk, salt, pepper, garlic powder, poultry seasoning, paprika and hot sauce. Set aside.

To make the chicken, place the chicken wings in a large freezer bag. Pour the brine into the bag, close and place in the fridge. Let it sit for at least 3 hours and up to 2 days. Add the flour, salt, pepper, paprika, garlic powder, cayenne pepper and poultry seasoning to a shallow dish and mix to combine. Working in batches, and using tongs, take the chicken wings out of the brine and drop them into the flour. Press the chicken into the flour to coat completely. Shake off the excess flour and place the chicken on a separate baking sheet. Repeat with the remaining chicken. Place the oil in a large Dutch oven and over medium-high heat (about 350°F [180°C]). Carefully, working in batches, add several pieces of chicken to the Dutch oven. Cook for 7 minutes, turning occasionally, until golden brown. Place on a wire rack to drain.

To make the waffles, in a medium bowl, whisk together the flour, sugar, nutmeg, cinnamon, baking powder, salt and baking soda. In a large bowl, whisk the eggs, vanilla and ricotta just to incorporate. Add the sweet potato juice and buttermilk to the egg mixture and whisk until smooth. Whisk in the melted brown butter, and then lightly fold the dry ingredients into the wet. Let the batter sit uncovered at room temperature for at least 20 minutes.

Preheat the oven to its lowest temperature setting and place a wire rack inside. Heat a waffle iron and spray it with nonstick spray. Pour about 1 cup (240 ml) of batter onto the waffle iron and cook for 5 to 7 minutes. Once done, lift the top and brush the waffle with a stick of butter. Apparently, this buttering method is somewhat controversial, but that's how I do mine. Transfer to the wire rack in the oven to keep warm. Repeat with the remaining batter. Serve with the chicken and that amazeballs Maple Bourbon Sauce.

BLACKENED SHRIMP AND FRIED POLENTA

This is my cool little take (at least I think so) on the classic shrimp and grits dish. I love this recipe because the grits, I mean the polenta, has this great crispy texture to it. I am all about texture. I think that's why I probably don't eat eggs, which is a story in and of itself. I mean why are those things always so saggy? Anyway, the shrimp in this recipe gets a great dose of flavor from the blackening spice, and then they're laid atop that deliciously cheesy, buttery and crispy fried polenta. Sounds great, right?!

For the Polenta

1 qt (960 ml) water

½ tsp salt

½ beef bouillon cube

1 cup (240 g) polenta

2 tbsp (28 g) butter

2 cups (226 g) shredded sharp Cheddar cheese

1 stick cold butter, for frying

For the Shrimp

1½ lbs (680 g) shrimp

1 tsp Blackening Spice (page 140)

¼ cup (60 ml) olive oil, divided

1 cup (160 g) diced yellow onion

½ cup (75 g) chopped green bell pepper

1 tsp salt

½ tsp pepper

½ tsp cayenne pepper

¼ tsp dried thyme

3 cloves garlic, minced

1 qt (960 ml) shrimp stock (see page 139) (may substitute with seafood stock)

¼ cup (60 ml) half-and-half

2 tbsp (6 g) finely chopped green onion

2 tbsp (8 g) chopped parsley

To make the polenta, grease a 7 x 11–inch (18 x 28–cm) baking dish with olive oil and set aside. Place the water in a large pot and bring it to a boil. Add the salt and whisk in the bouillon cube until it dissolves. Whisk in the polenta and cook, stirring frequently, until the water is almost absorbed, about 15 minutes. Stir in the butter and cheese and cook for 5 minutes, or until thickened. Pour the polenta into the greased baking dish and refrigerate until cool, about 2 hours.

Preheat the oven to 225°F (110°C).

Using a rubber spatula, free the edges of the polenta from the dish. Place a cutting board on top of the dish and invert to remove it from the pan. Slice the polenta into strips about 1 inch (2.5 cm) thick, and then again down the center. Place a heavy skillet over medium-high heat, and rub a cold stick of butter across it to grease it. Working in batches, place the polenta in the skillet and fry until golden brown, about 4 minutes on each side. Remove and place on a baking sheet in the oven while cooking the remaining batches.

To make the shrimp, season the shrimp with the Blackening Spice and set aside. Add 2 tablespoons (30 ml) of the olive oil to a large saucepan and place over medium heat. Add the onion, bell pepper, salt, pepper, cayenne and dried thyme. Cook for 3 minutes, or until soft. Add the garlic and cook for 1 minute. Add the shrimp stock and cook for 5 minutes. Stir in the half-and-half, green onion and parsley and simmer on low for 5 minutes. While that's simmering, add the remaining olive oil to a clean pan over medium-high heat. Add the shrimp and cook for 2 to 3 minutes on each side, or until they turn opaque. Serve by placing the shrimp over the fried polenta and then pouring the sauce over both. High five yourself.

BLUEBERRY CORN PANCAKES

While I may have just professed my love for waffles, don't get it twisted. I'll still get down with some pancakes. Especially corn pancakes. Just the small addition of some cornmeal changes the whole texture and flavor of what is probably America's favorite breakfast sweet. Throw in some delicious blueberries and fresh rosemary and your day's gotten off to a great start. I don't want to be the boss of you, but I highly recommend using honey instead of syrup with these pancakes. Honey pairs better with the delicate flavors and won't overpower it like syrup. Think of it this way: Would you put syrup on cornbread? Don't answer that.

1½ cups (188 g) all-purpose flour

1½ cups (183 g) cornmeal

2 tbsp (30 g) granulated sugar

2 tbsp (28 g) baking powder

1 tsp baking soda

½ tsp salt

1 tsp chopped fresh rosemary

2 large eggs

¼ cup (60 ml) melted butter

½ tbsp (8 ml) vanilla extract

2¼ cups (540 ml) milk, room temperature

1 stick cold butter, for greasing

2 cups (296 g) blueberries

Honey, for serving

Preheat the oven to 200°F (95°C).

In a large bowl, sift the flour, cornmeal, sugar, baking powder, baking soda and salt. Mix in the rosemary.

In a separate large bowl, whisk together the eggs, melted butter, vanilla and milk until just combined. Do not overmix. Gently fold the dry ingredients into the wet mixture until combined.

Place a cast-iron skillet on the stove over medium heat. Rub butter over a 3-inch (8-cm) circle in the skillet to grease the pan. Pour about 3 tablespoons (45 ml) of batter into the butter, and then drop a few blueberries in. Cook the first side until bubbles appear over most of the surface, and then flip. Continue to cook until the edges begin to look dry and the bottoms are golden brown, 5 to 6 minutes, total. Transfer to the oven until you're ready to get your pancake on. Serve with warm honey. I repeat: Serve with warm honey. You might be tempted to use syrup, but you don't want to overpower the delicate flavors that are dancing around in these delicious flapjacks.

AVOCADO TOAST WITH PECAN SMOKED CHICKEN

I've put just about anything you can think of on avocado toast on my Instagram feed. Soft-shell crab, ceviche, even fried chicken skin and watermelon. So I'd be remiss if I didn't include at least one avo toast recipe in this book. If you've made the Pecan Smoked Chicken with Alabammy White Sauce (which of course you have, page 47) and you have leftover, this little number is incredibly quick and delicious. It's so good that I've actually added it to my private chef menu as an appetizer. The smoky chicken topped with that incredible white BBQ sauce all atop cheesy buttered toast and avocado? It really is one delicious bite.

3–4 pieces Pecan Smoked Chicken (page 47)

2 pieces sourdough bread

Melted butter, as desired

2–4 slices provolone cheese

2 ripe avocados

¼ tsp kosher salt

Alabama White Barbecue Sauce (page 135)

I prefer dark meat for this dish 'cause as the kids say, "it just hits different." Remove the chicken from the bone if you've used bone-in. If you've used boneless, just give it a rough chop. Place the chicken in a small saucepan or in the microwave to warm it up. Take a couple of pieces of sourdough and toast them on both sides. Once toasted, brush with butter and top with enough provolone cheese to cover the bread. Place under a broiler to melt the cheese.

While the cheese is melting, slice open the avocados and place in a bowl. Mash the avocado with a fork and sprinkle with the salt. Spread the avocado over the melted cheese and top that with some of the chopped chicken. Drizzle some of the Alabama White Sauce on top, and there you have it. Easy-peasy deliciousness.

SOUL SIDES

I called this chapter Soul Sides for lack of a better term, but these dishes are nobody's side squeeze. All of these items have a depth of flavor and the character to stand on their own and go toe-to-toe with all types of cuisine. In fact, some of the most iconic soul food dishes are considered side items. Take my Almost Momma's Mac and Cheese (page 97), for example. This homestyle baked version provides a texture and flavor that just cannot be achieved on a stovetop with a couple of breadcrumbs. Another one of my favorites, the Fried Green Tomatoes with Oscar-Style Crab (page 110), is just bursting with unique and satisfying flavor. The crisp, ever-so-slightly sweet green tomatoes play deliciously well with the savory, somewhat decadent crab sauce. One of the dishes that truly surprised me in the making of this book was the Stewed Okra and Tomatoes (page 109). This dish blew me away with its simplicity and deliciousness. Not only is it equally as delicious in vegetarian form, but adding just a bit of rice makes this dish a healthy, quick and delicious meal.

MAKE YA HOLLA COLLARD GREENS

There are not many dishes that represent soul food better than collard greens. Loose-leafed cultivars of Brassica oleracea usually slow simmered with a big ole hunk of pork for flavor . . . although my recipe uses smoked turkey to provide that rich flavor, as I don't dine on the swine. I guess since we're getting to know each other, now is a good time to explain how and why I jettisoned Peppa and her people. I was fifteen years old, reading the teachings of Malcolm X and decided to live a "clean" and disciplined lifestyle. Of course, I still indulged in frequent consumption of honeybuns, soda and candy along with an occasional 40-ounce (1.2-L) of malt liquor, so "clean living" may not be completely accurate.

Anywho, fast-forward about eight years when I decided to get back on the trotter train. I settled myself in one evening in my dorm room and ordered a large meat lovers' pizza. I poured myself a nice cold glass of the finest malt liquor and enjoyed every porky piece of pie. About seven hours later, that pizza was violently trying to exit my body in every way imaginable and wasn't taking no for an answer. I spent the next several days in my bed in the fetal position and swore off swine from that day forth. You'll see smoked turkey often used as my swine sub, but please feel free to use ham hocks instead, no judgment.

2 qt (2 L) water

2 smoked turkey legs or ham hocks

6 cloves garlic, mashed

1 medium onion, sliced

2 tbsp (30 g) creole seasoning

2 tsp (4 g) ground black pepper

½ tsp garlic powder

½ tsp paprika

¼ tsp cayenne pepper

2 bay leaves

2 lbs (907 g) collard greens, washed, with tough stems discarded and chopped

1 qt (960 ml) chicken broth

2 tbsp (30 ml) pepper sauce

4 pickled peppers

Add the water, turkey, garlic, onion, creole seasoning, pepper, garlic powder, paprika, cayenne and bay leaves to a pot and bring it to a boil. Add the greens and stir to combine. Return the pot to a boil, and then reduce the heat to medium-low and simmer, partially covered, for 1½ hours, stirring occasionally.

Add the chicken broth and return the pot to a boil. Turn the heat down to medium-low and simmer for 1 hour, partially covered. The collards should be tender but still hold their shape. Turn off the heat, stir in the pepper sauce and pickled peppers, remove the bay leaves and serve.

FRIED OKRA

Love, love, love me some fried okra. Maybe it's that amazing okra texture combined with the crispy battered outside. Maybe it's the fact that I'm eating my veggies but still enjoying a tasty fried treat. Maybe it's because okra gets a bad rap in some circles, and I feel like I'm doing it a solid.

One thing you will observe during the fried food adventure of this book is that very few of my fry batters are the same. One pet peeve of mine is when I go to a restaurant and every fried item is coated in the same batter. Should the okra taste like the catfish, which tastes like the fried pickles, which tastes like the fried chicken? I think not and feel that you're doing each item a disservice by doing so. However, I realize that they're running a bitness and creating a different batter for each item can be incredibly time consuming.

You, however, are probably not cranking out commercial quantities of fried foods, and I will therefore provide a batter tailored specifically for each item. Like this recipe for fried okra. You're going to add just a little ole bitty scooch of sugar to that fry to complement the okra's natural sweetness. Would you want sugar on your catfish? Prolly not. But in your okra, hmm. . . . Now I've piqued your interest.

1 cup (125 g) all-purpose flour

½ cup (61 g) cornmeal

2 tsp (12 g) kosher salt, plus extra for serving

½ tsp onion powder

½ tsp paprika

½ tsp freshly ground black pepper

¼ tsp cayenne pepper

¼ tsp sugar

1 egg

1 cup (240 ml) milk

1 tbsp (15 ml) hot sauce

12 oz (340 g) okra, stems removed, sliced into ½" (1-cm)-thick rounds

Vegetable oil, for frying

Creole Buttermilk Ranch (page 144)

In a pie plate or paper lunch bag, mix together the flour, cornmeal, salt, onion powder, paprika, pepper, cayenne and sugar. Beat the egg in a small bowl, and then whisk in the milk and hot sauce. Working in batches, place the okra in the flour mixture to coat. Then remove it from the flour and place it in the egg mixture. Remove it from the egg and place it back in the flour one mo' 'gin to coat well.

Pour about 1 inch (2.5 cm) of vegetable oil into a large cast-iron skillet or Dutch oven and heat until it reaches 350°F (180°C).

Carefully place a single layer of okra in the oil, cooking for 2 to 3 minutes, or until golden brown, flipping halfway through. Using a slotted spoon, remove the okra to a wire rack or paper towel–lined plate. Sprinkle the okra with salt and serve with the Creole Buttermilk Ranch.

GREEN BEANS AND POTATOES

Another Southern vegetable staple, green beans were one of my favorite veggies to eat growing up. They were also the source of one of my first "cultural awakenings." I was probably around eight or nine years old and was playing over at a friend's house when his mother asked if I'd like to stay for dinner. I asked what we were having, and she said, "Chicken, green beans and rice." "Oooh, I love green beans," I exclaimed. When my plate arrived at the table, the beans that came with it were not the beans I knew and loved. They were bright green, crunchy and had little skinny nuts on them. Worst of all, to my horror, there were no potatoes! As I was raised to do, I choked down those crunchy ass beans and the rest of my meal with a smile. I did not, however, accept any more dinner invitations from this family.

Fortunately, since then, I have learned to appreciate green beans in all their varieties. As with all my recipes, feel free to ad-lib a bit here and there to your particular taste. Although, I feel they provide an extra heartiness to this dish, feel free to leave out the potatoes if you so choose. Although I implore you, please, please, no skinny nuts.

2 lbs (907 g) green beans

5 cloves garlic, mashed

1 smoked turkey leg or ham hock

1 medium onion, chopped

3 qt (3 L) chicken stock

¼ tsp onion powder

½ tsp garlic powder

½ tsp paprika

1 bay leaf

2 tsp (12 g) seasoned salt

2 russet potatoes, peeled and chopped into 2" (5-cm) cubes and placed in a bowl of cold water

Wash the green beans, snap off the ends and snap them into two pieces.

In a large pot, add the garlic, turkey leg, onion, chicken stock, onion powder, garlic powder, paprika, bay leaf and salt and bring to a boil over high heat. Place the beans in the pot, cover it slightly and reduce the heat to medium-low. Simmer the beans for 1 hour, stirring occasionally. If the beans are exposed, add some water to the pot to keep them covered. Add the potatoes and simmer for 30 minutes. Remove the bay leaf. The beans should be tender but still hold their shape.

ALMOST MOMMA'S MAC AND CHEESE

This recipe is dear to me as this was a family favorite around the holiday time. Now mind you, my relationship with this recipe wasn't always so rosy. As a small child, I was allergic to everything: eggs, cheese, chocolate, citrus . . . everything. Eventually, I grew out of most of them, but these early childhood allergies made me a very picky eater.

With the holiday table set, oohs and aahs would always accompany my mother's six-egg (I would later dub it "mac and quiche"), decadent mac and cheese when it arrived at the table. Except for me, that is. Scarred from my previous allergy, I hated eggs and would be waiting on my box mac and cheese, thank you very much. It wasn't until one fateful holiday when I came home after a full day of getting my "outside childhood boy" on that my eyes and palate finally saw the glory. With nothing else to eat but the previous night's mac and cheese and hungry enough to gnaw my own arm off, I finally gave in and tried this family favorite. It. Was. Glorious. Still waaaaaay too eggy, but delicious, nonetheless. And from there began my foray into finally eating "grown folks' food."

Not long after, I tried my hand at making it myself, reducing the egregious six eggs down to two and incorporating cheese soup, garlic and butter. The soup ensures you get cheese in every bite, while the garlic is added to melted butter just to wake it up a bit before adding it to the mix. It may not be momma's mac and quiche, but it definitely draws oohs and aahs when I bring it to the table.

2 tbsp (28 g) butter

1 clove garlic, minced

1 qt (960 ml) milk, plus some extra

2 eggs

2 (10.5-oz [298-g]) cans Cheddar cheese soup

2 tsp (4 g) ground black pepper

2 tsp (10 g) creole seasoning

3½ cups (700 g) large elbow macaroni, cooked al dente

4 cups (452 g) shredded Colby Jack cheese, divided

Dash of paprika

NOTE: This mac and cheese can be made two ways. If you're going for the traditional firmer version, cook for 25 to 30 minutes. As it cools, it will firm up, so don't cook it too long or it will be dry. If you prefer a cheese sauce mac and cheese, take it out after 20 to 22 minutes. Don't post that version on the Gram though, as baked mac and cheese purists will shame you for it being too runny.

Preheat the oven to 375°F (190°C).

Melt the butter in a saucepan over medium-low heat. Turn off the heat and add the garlic. Swirl it around in the pan for 15 seconds, or just long enough to wake it up and have someone say "Mmmm, smells good in here." Add the garlic and butter to a large bowl with the milk, eggs, Cheddar cheese soup, pepper and creole seasoning. Mix with a hand mixer or whisk until fully incorporated, about 2 minutes.

Add some of the pasta to a 2-quart (2-L) baking dish, spreading to even it out until the pasta comes about halfway up the sides of the dish. (There'll probably be pasta left over. No one, including me, really knows how much pasta to actually cook.) Add the cheese mixture and 2 cups (226 g) of the shredded cheese and mix together with a spoon. The mixture should be fairly liquidy. If it looks too thick, add a bit more milk and mix again. Smooth the mixture over with a spoon, making sure all of the noods are covered in the cheese sauce. Sprinkle the remaining shredded cheese on top, and ever so gently spread with a spoon top to make sure it's distributed evenly. Give this awesome dish of cheese and noods a light dusting of paprika.

Place the mac and cheese in the oven on the middle rack for approximately 22 to 25 minutes. Take a quick peek around 20 minutes as you don't want to overcook it. You want your M&C silky and cheesy, not dry AF. The mac and cheese is done when the top just begins to brown. Remove from the oven and let it cool for 5 minutes to help it set. Proceed to eat your amazing mac and cheese till you get the cheese sweats and have to unbutton your pants and lie on your side.

GULLAH RED RICE

Gullah red rice is one of the special recipes that helped me rediscover my family history when researching for this book. I grew up in the Midwest in Detroit, Michigan, but my mother was raised in Savannah, Georgia, and the foods she grew up with were a large part of our diet. As part of the low country, the coastal region of Georgia and South Carolina between the two Jacksonvilles (not to be confused with the Low Country, the counties of Beaufort, Colleton, Hampton and Jasper in South Carolina), several traditional dishes from Savannah involve rice, which at one time was the dominant crop of the region (as is the case with many crops associated with soul food). Enslaved Africans brought with them the knowledge of how to grow the crops as well as their recipes of how to prepare them. My mother would start off frying up several strips of bacon. She'd pour just a bit of the bacon grease off, and then add all of her ingredients (sans Worcestershire, sugar and tomato paste) to her magical Pyrex pot. A short time later, she would emerge with this fluffy red rice that was always a family favorite. While this recipe is not exactly how my momma made it, it still brings back memories of my mother placing that big Pyrex dish on the table and removing the glass top to reveal a steaming hot, delicious pot of red rice.

12 oz (340 g) smoked sausage, diced, or 4 strips of bacon

3 cups (720 ml) chicken stock

2 tbsp (30 g) tomato paste

1 medium yellow onion, chopped

1 large green bell pepper, chopped

1 tbsp (9 g) minced garlic

2 tsp (12 g) kosher salt, plus more to taste

1 tsp granulated sugar

1 tsp Worcestershire sauce

2 (14.5-oz [411-g]) cans stewed tomatoes

¼ tsp cayenne pepper

½ tsp black pepper

2 cups (400 g) long-grain rice, rinsed until water runs clear

Sliced scallion greens, for serving

Preheat the oven to 350°F (180°C) and coat a 9 x 13–inch (23 x 33–cm) baking dish with cooking spray.

Add the sausage or bacon to a large heavy skillet and fry over medium heat until browned, 2 to 3 minutes on each side. Remove from the skillet, leaving the rendered fat behind. Add the chicken stock to a medium-size bowl and whisk in the tomato paste. Add the onion and bell pepper to the skillet and sauté for 4 to 5 minutes, or until the onion is translucent. Add the garlic and sauté for 30 seconds. Add the salt, sugar, Worcestershire, stewed tomatoes, cayenne, pepper and sausage or bacon. Simmer for 5 minutes, breaking up some of the tomatoes with a spoon as you go.

Add the rice and bring everything to a boil. Reduce the heat to low and simmer for 5 minutes. Carefully transfer the ingredients to the greased baking dish and cover with foil. Bake until the rice is tender, 35 to 45 minutes. Fluff with a fork, garnish with sliced scallion greens and serve up some low-country goodness.

PIMENTO CHEESE HUSH PUPPIES

Pimento cheese . . . a dish so Southern it feels like you should be eating it in a rocking chair on the front porch during a hot summer day, dabbing the sweat from your brow as you wave to your neighbor while enjoying an ice-cold lemonade. It wasn't until I started testing out this recipe that I discovered how truly polarizing pimento cheese is. As someone who gave himself the nickname Cheezy F. Baby, of course I could eat a tub of the stuff, but others were not so enthused. Fortunately, in this recipe, this love-or-hate cheese is clandestinely hidden inside a delicious, crispy hush puppy. So maybe just serve it up and let someone accidentally discover they actually love the stuff. This recipe is a bit of a two-for-one as you are quite welcome to simply make the pimento and enjoy it by itself as well as the hush puppies.

For the Pimento Cheese

2¼ cups (254 g) shredded extra-sharp Cheddar cheese

¼ tsp paprika

¼ tsp minced garlic

2 tbsp (28 g) softened salted butter

½ cup (116 g) cream cheese, softened

3 tbsp (45 ml) mayonnaise

1 (14-oz [397-g]) jar diced pimento, drained

¼ tsp black pepper

Salt, to taste

For the Hush Puppies

1½ cups (183 g) fine- or medium-grind cornmeal

½ cup (63 g) all-purpose flour

1½ tsp (9 g) kosher salt

1½ tsp (7 g) baking powder

½ tsp baking soda

¼ tsp paprika

¼ tsp garlic powder

¼ tsp cayenne pepper

½ small yellow onion

1 tbsp (3 g) chopped green onion

1 large egg

2 tbsp (30 ml) melted butter

1 cup (240 ml) buttermilk

3 cups (720 ml) peanut or vegetable oil, for deep frying

To make the pimento cheese, in a medium bowl, mix together the Cheddar cheese, paprika, garlic, butter, cream cheese, mayo, pimento, pepper and salt. Place in a container and set aside in the refrigerator.

To make the hush puppies, in a large bowl, whisk together the cornmeal, flour, salt, baking powder, baking soda, paprika, garlic powder and cayenne. Grate the onion on the largest holes of a box grater and add to the bowl. Add the green onion, egg, butter and buttermilk and mix to combine.

Remove the pimento cheese from the fridge. Using a large spoon, scoop out about ¼ cup (60 g) of the hush puppy batter and flatten into a disk. Place 1 tablespoon (8 g) of the cheese in the middle of the batter and form the batter around the cheese until there is no cheese exposed. This should make six to eight large hush puppies, each about 3 inches (8 cm) in diameter. Set aside on parchment paper for 10 minutes to rest while the oil heats.

Add the oil to a Dutch oven or large skillet and heat over medium-high heat. Once hot, drop balls of batter into the oil, three to four at a time, to avoid crowding the pot. Cook for 3 to 4 minutes, turning occasionally, until golden brown on all sides. Remove with a slotted spoon and drain on a wire rack or paper towels. Repeat with the remaining batter. Serve to one of your pimento-hatin' friends and post their reaction on the internets.

PICKLED SHRIMP

Anyone who knows me or follows me on the Gram knows that I am a shrimp connoisseur. A shrimp sommelier, if you will. A man that loves shrimps so much I think I'm giving myself a new nickname: Scotty Gump. Broiled, fried, gumboed, blackened, coconutted or any other way I can eat it I'll take it. Surprisingly enough, though, up until fairly recently, I had never pickled these delicious little sea creatures. Oh, for shame. If you've never had pickled shrimp, you're in for a real treat. Served cold, they are cool and refreshing and provide a delicious twang that makes you pucker up and come back for more. One reason I love this recipe so much is that this is a make-ahead, toss-in-the-fridge, easy-peasy little number you can make the day before when you're havin' folks over or havin' "cumpnee," as it's said in some parts of the country.

BONUS ALERT! You can actually combine this with another recipe for a funky little twist. Keep a-readin' for more information.

½ medium onion, thinly sliced

1 lemon, thinly sliced

4 bay leaves

¾ cup (180 ml) cider vinegar

½ cup (120 ml) extra-virgin olive oil

2 Fresno chili peppers, sliced

½ habanero pepper, sliced

¼ cup (60 g) capers with their juice

½ tsp celery seeds

½ tsp sugar

½ tsp salt

1 tsp chopped fresh dill

1½ lbs (680 g) cooked and peeled shrimp

Take all this stuff—the onion, lemon slices, bay leaves, cider vinegar, oil, Fresno peppers, habanero pepper, capers, celery seeds, sugar, salt, dill and shrimp—and put it in a freezer bag. Massage said bag as if it's had a hard day at work. Throw your bag of shrimp goodies in the fridge for 24 hours. Remove from the fridge and place in a bowl. Remove the bay leaves and enjoy. Thank me.

Now here's the bonus: Sometimes I will omit the pepper sauce and peppers from the Make Ya Holla Collard Greens (page 90) and sprinkle a couple of these delicious shrimpies on top of the greens. They serve the same purpose as the peppers except they're skrimps! #mindblownemoji. Just make sure to add them once the greens have already been plated. The shrimp are already cooked and pickled, and adding them to the hot pot will overcook them.

APPLES AND SWEET POTATOES

As one of the soul food superheroes, you will find sweet potatoes scattered throughout this book. As a replacement for the yams that were grown in Africa, sweet potatoes were a staple in the diet of enslaved Africans. This particular dish is one of my favorites from my mother's recipes. The sweetness of the apples and sweet potatoes made me feel like I was cheating and getting an extra dessert during dinner. In this variation, I've added just a touch of curry for an extra level of flavor to this already incredible dish. These are delicious any time of the year, but because of the different spices and warmth, they feel extra special in the fall and winter months.

For the Sweet Potatoes

3 large sweet potatoes

Olive oil, for drizzling

¼ tsp cinnamon

¼ tsp curry

¼ tsp salt

3 tbsp (45 ml) melted butter

1 tsp vanilla extract

1 tsp honey

½ cup (120 ml) milk

For the Apples

3 tbsp (42 g) butter

4 apples (preferably Honeycrisp, Braeburn or Gala) cored, peeled and sliced in ¼" (6-mm) slices

3 tbsp (38 g) cinnamon sugar (2 tbsp [30 g] sugar, 1 tbsp [8 g] cinnamon)

Freshly squeezed lemon juice, as needed

Preheat the oven to 425°F (220°C).

To make the sweet potatoes, peel the potatoes and chop them into large chunks. Place the potatoes on a baking sheet, drizzle with olive oil and then toss to coat. Bake for 15 to 20 minutes. Flip the potatoes and cook for 10 to 15 minutes, or until a fork can easily pass through the center. Place the sweet potatoes in a bowl and mash with a fork. Add the cinnamon, curry, salt, butter, vanilla, honey and milk and blend with a hand mixer until smooth and fluffy.

To make the apples, place the butter in a cast-iron skillet or large pan over medium heat. Once the butter has melted, add one layer of sliced apples. Sprinkle the apples with about half of the cinnamon sugar. Cook for 2 minutes, and then flip and cook for 2 minutes. Squeeze some lemon juice over the apples, remove them from the pan along with any butter and set aside. Repeat with the remaining apples.

Place the apples in a baking dish and pour the butter from the pan over top. Top with the sweet potato mixture and place in the oven for 10 minutes, or until the tops of the sweet potato mixture begin to brown. Remove from the oven and serve warm.

HOT WATER CORNBREAD

This recipe is one of my favorites for its pure simplicity and minimal ingredients. Usually, whenever I create a recipe, I'm trying to add a tweak here or a tweak there to "make it my own." For this recipe, however, I ignored every fiber of my being that was whispering in my ear, "Scotty, get funky with it. Maybe a little duck fat, maybe some cheese, maybe just a little butter . . ." Nope, nope, and that's a no for me, dawg. I even resisted the urge to add baking powder to help the cornbread rise. Many recipes call for elaborate ingredients and numerous steps in the process, but once again, the beauty here is in the simplicity.

"Hot water" or "scald meal" cornbread is unique to the American South. According to several historians, hot water cornbread is "aboriginal cornbread," or what Native Americans were eating prior to settlers' arrival, and was passed along or shared with enslaved Africans. It was perfect in that it required very few ingredients, which fit well with the make-do-with-what-you-have recipes of enslaved Africans. Cornbread and its varieties were ideal for slaves who worked in the fields, because it did not require utensils, could be easily transported and could last a long time. Not only do I feel like I'm eating a piece of history when eating hot water cornbread, but I love the surprising-yet-not-so-surprising similarity to one of my favorite foods: tacos. That's right, tacos. For anyone that's ever made tortillas from scratch, you know the basic ingredients, and therefore underlying flavor, are exactly the same: corn, salt and hot or warm water. While not suitable for tacos in this form, hot water cornbread is delicious with butter or for sopping up pot-liquor from those delicious greens you made on page 90. And just think, next time you see someone making some corn tortillas, you can tell them, "Aw, man that ain't nothin' but some skinny-ass hot water cornbread."

2 cups (244 g) cornmeal

1½ tsp (9 g) salt

1½ cups (360 ml) boiling water

2 cups (480 ml) corn oil

Add the cornmeal and salt to a medium-size bowl and whisk to combine. Add the boiling water and stir until combined. Add the oil to a cast-iron skillet and heat over medium-high heat until the temperature reaches around 350°F (180°C).

Form the batter into 3-inch (8-cm) patties and carefully drop them into the oil. Fry for 4 to 5 minutes, turning once until both sides are golden. Remove from the oil and place on a wire rack or paper towel to drain.

STEWED OKRA AND TOMATOES

As I mentioned in the intro to this chapter, this dish really blew me away while I worked on it. The simplicity, the flavors and textures, and the different variations (vegetarian or maybe add some shrimp) make this one of my new faves. Now here's the kicker: I have only recently become a fan of okra. In fact, my gumbo recipe does not include okra because I used to dislike it and didn't want to change what I still feel is a darn good recipe. This recipe, which was created specifically for this book, is part of what I call my "low-country awakening." This is one of the recipes that I can trace through my own family history but had totally overlooked throughout my cooking journey. And so now I present to you a delicious dish that is easy to make and loaded with cultural significance.

3 tbsp (42 g) duck fat, unsalted butter, lard or bacon drippings

1 medium yellow onion, chopped

½ orange bell pepper, chopped

1 tbsp (9 g) minced garlic

12 oz (340 g) fresh okra, washed, trimmed and cut into ½" (1.3-cm)-thick slices

2 cups (360 g) chopped ripe tomatoes

1 cup (240 ml) chicken stock

¼ tsp cayenne pepper

½ tsp salt

½ tsp black pepper

1 tsp chopped fresh thyme

1 bay leaf

Rice, for serving (optional)

Place the duck fat in a large pot over medium heat. Once the duck fat has melted, add the onion and bell pepper and cook for 3 minutes, or until the veggies begin to soften.

Add the garlic and cook for 2 minutes, or until the garlic becomes fragrant. Add the okra, tomatoes, stock, cayenne, salt, black pepper, thyme and bay leaf. Stir and cook for 20 minutes, or until the okra becomes tender. Remove the bay leaf. Serve as a side or over rice, if desired.

FRIED GREEN TOMATOES WITH OSCAR-STYLE CRAB

Welp! Here we are again with another cornmeal and flour-battered dish and exhibit A of why I like to change up my fry mixtures. What I omitted from my previous rant about the one-size-fits-all fry mixture (see page 93) is that it ultimately has to do with the seasonings you're dropping in that mixture. Adding each spice individually allows you to control exactly how your dish is going to taste. Additionally, it avoids the dreaded possibility of your favorite spice blend being out of stock at the supermarket. Just imagine, you're throwing a big shindig and inviting all of your friends over. You go to the store for your favorite seasoning and they're all out! Here we'll be mixing up another delicious fry for one of my favorite Southern delicacies, fried green tomatoes, fancied up a bit with some Oscar-style crab meat. Deliciously light and slightly sweet green tomatoes fried up to a crispy golden brown topped with a lumpity, lump, lump crabmeat sauce that makes every bite a symphony of flavors.

For the Tomatoes

4 large green tomatoes, sliced

1 cup (125 g) all-purpose flour

1 cup (122 g) cornmeal

2 tsp (12 g) coarse kosher salt

½ tsp freshly ground black pepper

¼ tsp garlic powder

¼ tsp onion powder

¼ tsp cayenne pepper

½ tsp paprika

2 eggs, beaten

½ cup (120 ml) milk

3 cups (720 ml) vegetable oil

For the Crab

3 tbsp (42 g) butter

1 small onion, diced

¼ cup (25 g) diced celery

1 tbsp (9 g) minced garlic

1 lb (454 g) crabmeat

1 tsp hot sauce, or to taste

¼ tsp Worcestershire sauce

2 tbsp (30 ml) freshly squeezed lemon juice

½ tsp salt

¼ tsp freshly ground black pepper

¼ cup (60 ml) mayonnaise

To prepare the tomatoes, place the tomato slices in a single layer on doubled-up paper towels and let rest for 10 minutes.

Place the flour, cornmeal, salt, pepper, garlic powder, onion powder, cayenne and paprika on a plate and mix to combine. In a shallow bowl, whisk together the eggs and milk. Dredge the tomato slices in the cornmeal mixture, then into the egg wash and then back into the cornmeal mixture. Don't be afraid to give the tomatoes a light mash into the cornmeal to make sure it sticks. Place the tomatoes on a baking sheet.

Pour the oil into a deep 12-inch (30-cm) skillet over medium-high heat until the oil reaches a temperature of 350°F (180°C). Fry the tomatoes in batches to avoid overcrowding the pan. Fry for 4 to 5 minutes total, gently turning as needed until golden brown on both sides. Remove the tomatoes from the oil using a slotted spoon and place on a wire rack or paper towel. Do not stack.

To make the crab, melt the butter in a medium skillet over medium heat. Add the onion and cook over medium-low heat for 3 to 5 minutes, or until the pieces begin to soften. Add the celery and cook for 2 to 3 minutes, or until the celery begins to soften. Add the garlic and cook for 30 seconds, or until fragrant. Add the crabmeat, hot sauce, Worcestershire sauce, lemon juice, salt and pepper. Gently stir to combine, being careful not to break up the crab. Cook for 1 to 2 minutes, or until warmed throughout. Remove the crab pan from the heat and stir in the mayo. Serve over the top of those delicious fried green maters.

SWEET TOOTH

I've got what you might describe as a binge-y sweet tooth. I might go months without eating any sweets, and then Bam! I eat a whole damn pie in one day. The desserts I've compiled in this chapter would be the ones you'd normally be trying to decide between when rounding out your order at your favorite soul food restaurant. Fortunately for you, here you don't have to choose just one! You can work your way through them all. What will be the first one you make? Will it be the Praline Pecan Sweet Potato Pie (page 125)? This is decadence personified with its bourbon-scented pecan pie filling topped with light and airy sweet potato pie filling and finished off with praline pecan morsels. If you want layers of dessert decadence this is where you begin. Or maybe you want to start with something a bit more traditional like Peachy Keen Cobbler (page 121). Deliciously sweet peaches with just a hint of orange zest and a crust that will have you fighting for a corner piece. No matter where you begin, you really can't go wrong with any of these delicious

WORLD'S BEST SWEET POTATO PIE

Hands down, without a doubt, no question, this is my most prized recipe. Why? Well, it's the World's Best Sweet Potato Pie, of course. But mainly because it was my great-grandmother's recipe handed down to me from my mother. It brings me joy to know that a recipe created in a small kitchen in Georgia probably 100 years ago is now bringing sweet potato joy to people all over the world. The question is, how much side-eye will I get at the family reunion for giving this recipe away? Fingers crossed.

2 frozen deep-dish pie shells

4 large sweet potatoes

1 cup (226 g) butter

¼ cup (60 ml) half-and-half

½ cup (120 ml) evaporated milk (I prefer Carnation)

1⅔ cups (332 g) granulated sugar

4 extra-large eggs

2½ tbsp (38 ml) vanilla extract

¼ tsp cinnamon

¼ tsp nutmeg

¼ tsp salt

½ tsp key lime juice

Preheat the oven to 375°F (190°C). Remove the pie shells from the freezer to thaw just a bit.

Place a large pot of water to boil on the stove. Slice the sweet potatoes in half longwise and place in the boiling water. Boil the sweet taters until a fork can easily be pushed through the cut side, about 15 minutes.

While the taters are a boilin', add the butter to a bowl and microwave until melted. In a large bowl, add the melted butter, half-and-half, evaporated milk, sugar, eggs, vanilla, cinnamon, nutmeg and salt and mix with a hand mixer.

Remove the sweet potatoes from the water and drain. Using a clean dish towel, remove the skins, being careful not to burn your dainty little chef fingers. Add the taters to the bowl with the other ingredients and mix using the hand mixer. Add the key lime juice and mix to combine.

Prick each pie shell with a fork four to five times. Pricking holes in the pie dough allows the steam to escape while it's baking and avoids what I like to call the dreaded pimple pie. Pour the mixture into the shells. Bake the pies on the middle oven rack for 45 minutes, or until a toothpick inserted in the center comes out clean. Remove from the oven and place those gorgeous pies on a pie rack to cool for 1 hour. Behold the power you now possess as a baker of the World's Best Sweet Potato Pie.

RED "WHAT IS THIS VELVET?" CAKE

I love red velvet cake for the simple fact that I'm always sitting there eating it, thinking, "What in the heck am I eating? I taste a little chocolate. I taste a little vanilla. I see a lot of red, but it ain't strawberry." Ultimately, my brain is like, "I don't know what this is, but it sure is delicious." Swapping out olive oil for butter in this cake gives it a slightly nutty undertone, which I think pairs well with the small amount of cocoa powder used. Swap out a bit of the traditional cream cheese for Italian mascarpone for a super-smooth frosting, and you've got yourself one delicious cake.

For the Cake

2½ cups (313 g) all-purpose flour, plus more for dusting

1 tsp baking powder

1 tsp fine salt

1 tbsp (5 g) unsweetened cocoa powder

1 tsp espresso powder

1½ cups (360 ml) light olive oil

1½ cups (300 g) granulated sugar

2 large eggs, room temperature

1 tsp vanilla extract

1 cup (240 ml) low-fat buttermilk, room temperature

2 tbsp (30 ml) red gel food coloring

1 tbsp (15 ml) white distilled vinegar

1 tsp baking soda

For the Cream Cheese Frosting

8 oz (226 g) mascarpone, softened

½ cup (114 g) butter, softened

8 oz (226 g) cream cheese, softened

1 tsp vanilla extract

¼ tsp kosher salt

2 cups (240 g) confectioners' sugar

Preheat the oven to 350°F (180°C). Butter and flour two 9-inch (23-cm) cake pans.

To make the cake, in a large bowl, whisk together the flour, baking powder, salt, cocoa powder and espresso powder. In a medium bowl, add the olive oil and sugar. Beat with a hand mixer or an electric stand mixer. Add the eggs, one at a time, beating well after each one. Add the vanilla extract and beat until combined. Add the buttermilk and red food coloring. Mix to combine. With the mixer on low speed, alternate adding in the flour mixture to the liquid mixture, beginning and ending with the flour.

In a small cup, combine the vinegar and baking soda, and then quickly fold it into the cake batter. Divide the batter evenly between the two prepared pans. Bake for 25 minutes, or until a toothpick inserted into the center comes out clean. Cool the cakes for 10 minutes before inverting them onto a plate and then re-inverting onto an oiled wire rack to cool. Once the cakes have completely cooled, wrap in plastic and place in the refrigerator for a few hours to firm.

To make the cream cheese frosting, in the bowl of an electric stand mixer, beat the mascarpone, butter and cream cheese until smooth. Add the vanilla extract, salt and confectioners' sugar and beat until smooth and fluffy.

Spread one cake layer with a layer of frosting, and then place the second layer of cake on top of the frosting and frost the top and sides of the cake.

SALTED CARAMEL CAST-IRON BREAD PUDDING

I've never been a huge fan of bread pudding, but this one might make it into my regular rotation. Using a cast-iron skillet helps crisp up the bottom a bit, and the salted caramel sauce turns a fairly regular bread pudding into a truly decadent dessert. I had a piece with my coffee one morning and almost felt a bit guilty. Almost.

For the Pudding

1 tbsp (14 g) butter, plus more for greasing

2 cups (480 ml) whole milk

2 cups (480 ml) half-and-half

½ cup (110 g) packed brown sugar

¼ tsp salt

1 tbsp (15 ml) bourbon

1 tbsp (15 ml) vanilla extract

1 tsp ground cinnamon

¼ tsp ground nutmeg

3 large eggs, lightly beaten

1 loaf day-old challah bread, cubed into 2" (5-cm) pieces

For the Salted Caramel Sauce

1 cup (200 g) granulated sugar

7 tbsp (98 g) butter, room temperature, cut into cubes

1¼ cups (300 ml) heavy cream, room temperature

1 tsp salt

Preheat the oven to 350°F (180°C) and lightly butter a 9-inch (23-cm) cast-iron pan.

To make the pudding, in a small pot, add the milk, half-and-half, brown sugar, salt, bourbon and butter. Place over medium heat for 3 to 4 minutes, or until warmed and the butter is melted. Remove from the heat and set aside to allow it to cool slightly. Whisk in the vanilla, cinnamon and nutmeg, and then whisk in the eggs one at a time. Add the bread to the cast-iron pan. Pour the custard over the bread, making sure to get it in all the little cracks and holes. Let it sit for 10 to 15 minutes to allow the bread to soak up all the custard. Bake for 25 to 30 minutes, or until a knife inserted in the middle comes out clean. Since the cast-iron pan is a bit shallower than a standard baking dish, the cooking time will be shorter.

To make the caramel sauce, heat the sugar in a medium heavy-duty saucepan over medium heat, stirring constantly with a wooden spoon. Once the sugar has melted, stir in the butter until melted and combined. (If the butter starts separating from the sugar, remove the pan from the heat and vigorously whisk or stir to combine it again, before returning it to the heat.) After the butter has melted, let sit for 1 minute without stirring. Carefully stir in the heavy cream. After all the heavy cream has been added, stop stirring and allow it to boil for 1 minute. Remove from the heat and stir in the salt.

Slice the bread pudding from the middle out like you would a pie and place it on a plate. Drizzle with the caramel sauce.

PEACHY KEEN COBBLER

This cobbler is delicious, and you guys better make this thing 'cause when I was writing this book, peaches weren't in season and my deadline was looming and it was really stressing me out. Now that I've gotten that off my chest, is this a cobbler or a pie? While researching this important question, "biscuity crumbled topping" kept popping up. However, when I was growing up, my momma called this a cobbler. Are y'all calling my momma a liar? Anyway, all I know is my momma called it cobbler, so Ima call it cobbler. And with an incredible peach filling and amazing non-biscuity crust, you'll call it delicious.

For the Crust

2½ cups (313 g) all-purpose flour

½ cup (100 g) granulated sugar

¼ tsp salt

2 egg yolks

1½ tsp (8 ml) vanilla extract

1 cup (226 g) cold butter, cut into 1" (2.5-cm) cubes

¼ cup (60 ml) cold water

For the Filling

6 cups (3 kg) fresh peaches, peeled and sliced

¼ cup (57 g) unsalted butter

½ cup (100 g) granulated sugar

½ cup (110 g) brown sugar

½ tsp ground cinnamon

¼ tsp nutmeg

½ tsp orange zest

¼ tsp salt

1 tbsp (15 ml) vanilla extract

For the Egg Wash

1 egg, beaten with 2 tsp (10 ml) water

To make the crust, add to a medium bowl the flour, sugar and salt and whisk together to combine. Mix the egg yolks and vanilla together in a small bowl. Cut the butter into the flour using a food processor, fork or pastry cutter until various-sized crumbs appear. Add the egg yolks and vanilla and mix to combine. Slowly add the cold water into the flour and form it into a ball, and then quickly knead the dough to bring it together. Remove the dough from the bowl, cut it into two sections and round into balls. Flatten each ball into a disk, cover tightly with plastic wrap and place in the refrigerator for at least 35 minutes.

To make the filling, place the peaches, butter, sugar and brown sugar in a large pot over medium-high heat. Bring to a boil, and then reduce down to medium. Cook for 15 minutes, stirring occasionally to make sure they are combined. Turn off the heat and add the cinnamon, nutmeg, orange zest, salt and vanilla. Stir once again to combine, and then set aside.

Preheat the oven to 375°F (190°C).

Dust some flour on your work surface and remove the dough from the fridge. Unwrap one of the disks, and using a rolling pin, quickly roll the dough out to about a thickness of ⅓ inch (8 mm). Place the dough on the bottom and up the sides of a 9 x 13–inch (23 x 33–cm) baking dish. Carefully pour or spoon the peaches on top of the dough.

Roll out the second disk as you did the first. Using a pastry scraper or knife, cut the dough into 2-inch (5-cm)-wide strips. Carefully remove the strips from the countertop and place them on top of the cobbler. Brush the top of the dough with the egg wash, and then bake for 35 to 40 minutes, or until the crust is golden brown. Remove from the oven and place on a cooling rack for at least 2 hours before enjoying.

KENTUCKY BUTTER CAKE

During the first drafting of the recipes for this book, I had several cakes that, after comparing the ingredients, seemed to be variations of one another. My buttermilk lemon pound cake, marble pound cake and hot milk cake all seemed to be cousins if not siblings of one another and seemed a bit redundant to include in a book that wasn't just about cakes. I chose this one because it's delicious (of course), but also because I found it thumbing through my mother's old cookbook. Handwritten on a tattered piece of Detroit Public Schools pink stationary from my mother's many years as a high school counselor, this cake brought back a many great memories of my mother in the kitchen. I do have to warn you, though: this cake is incredibly addictive. The crispy glazed outside and crumbly moist interior will have you cutting your first slice, and then coming back for one more little piece, and one more little piece, and one more little piece.

For the Cake

1 cup (226 g) butter

2 cups (400 g) sugar

1 tsp rum extract

1½ tsp (8 ml) vanilla extract

4 eggs

3 cups (375 g) all-purpose flour

1 tsp baking powder

½ tsp baking soda

1¼ tsp (7 g) salt

1 cup (240 ml) buttermilk

For the Butter Sauce

¾ cup (150 g) granulated sugar

3 tbsp (45 ml) water

⅓ cup (75 g) butter

1 tsp vanilla extract

Preheat the oven to 325°F (165°C). Grease and flour a twelve-cup fluted tube pan.

To make the cake, in a large bowl, cream the butter and sugar until very creamy (almost white). Add the rum and vanilla. Add the eggs, one at a time and blend at low speed until moistened, about 3 minutes. In a medium bowl, sift the flour before measuring, and then measure and resift with the baking powder, baking soda and salt. Add the flour, a small amount at a time, to the butter mixture, alternating with the buttermilk and ending up with the flour mixture. Bake for 60 to 75 minutes, or until a toothpick inserted in the center comes out clean.

To make the butter sauce, place the sugar, water and butter in a medium saucepan over medium-low heat, and cook until the butter melts. Remove from the heat and stir in the vanilla. Pour over the hot cake and enjoy.

PRALINE PECAN SWEET POTATO PIE

I'm gonna let y'all in on a little controversial secret I have. *Whispers softly* For some pies, the crust really doesn't matter. Yeah, I said it. What do I mean by that? Well what I mean is, don't slave over a homemade piecrust unnecessarily for every pie you make. For some pies, the crust is extremely important. A peach "cobbler" would be a good example where in some households the crust is more important than the filling, and if the crust-to-filling ratio is off (too much crust) on your slice, there might be a kerfuffle about to go down. For other pies, namely those with no top crust, the crust is just a vessel for getting that delicious pie into your pie hole. This is one such pie. In fact, it is so decadently delicious that you could serve it on a flip-flop and it would still be amazing. All this to say, don't let someone crust shame you into making a crust from scratch for this pie. Premade will do just fine.

For the Filling and Crust

3 large eggs, beaten

½ cup (120 ml) light corn syrup

½ cup (120 ml) dark corn syrup

¼ cup (55 g) packed brown sugar

¼ cup (50 g) granulated sugar

¼ tsp salt

1 tsp vanilla extract

⅓ cup (75 g) unsalted butter

1 tsp bourbon

1 cup (109 g) chopped pecans

Sweet potato pie filling, from World's Best Sweet Potato Pie (page 114, see Note)

1 premade deep-dish piecrust

For the Pralines

1 cup (200 g) granulated sugar

1 cup (220 g) packed brown sugar

½ cup (120 ml) evaporated milk

5 tbsp (71 g) unsalted butter, cubed

1 tsp pure vanilla extract

½ tsp salt

1½ cups (164 g) coarsely chopped pecans

Preheat the oven to 350°F (180°C).

For the pie filling, in a large bowl, add the eggs, light corn syrup, dark corn syrup, brown sugar, granulated sugar, salt and vanilla and whisk to combine. Place the butter in a small saucepan over medium-low heat until melted. Add the bourbon and cook over low heat for 1 minute. Remove from the heat and allow to cool slightly before adding to the egg mixture. Stir to combine. Spread the pecans on the bottom of the piecrust. Pour just enough of the egg and syrup mixture over the pecans to cover them. The pecan mixture should fill about half of the crust. There will be some mixture left over.

Place the sweet potato batter in a piping bag. If you don't have a piping bag, you can place it in a larger freezer bag and cut one of the corners off to make a small piping hole. Starting at the outside edge and working your way around, carefully squeeze out the sweet potato pie batter onto the pecan pie filling. The goal is to keep the sweet potato pie filling on top and not allow the pecan pie filling to seep up from underneath. I used my kid's little bitty child medicine syringe to suck out some of the pecan filling around the edges. Use what works best for you. Bake for 50 minutes, or until a toothpick inserted into the middle comes out clean. When inserting the toothpick, you're only testing for the doneness of the sweet potato as the pecan will already be done, so you only need to insert it about halfway.

To make the pralines, place some parchment paper on top of a baking sheet. Add the granulated sugar, brown sugar and evaporated milk in a medium saucepan over medium heat. Stir until the contents are combined and all the sugar has dissolved. Remove from the heat and place the butter on top. Let it sit for 1 minute. Add the vanilla, salt and the pecans and stir continuously with a wooden spoon for 3 minutes, or until the candy begins to thicken. Drop spoonfuls of the candy onto the parchment paper and let it cool for 1 hour.

Once the pie is done and has cooled for at least 3 hours, it's time for the praline crumbles. Chop up some of the pralines and crumble them on top of the pie until the whole top is covered. Slice and enjoy.

NOTE: Reduce the sugar from 1⅔ cups (332 g) to ¾ cup (150 g), 'cause, you know, "big momma your arm."

NANA PUDDING

I'm not a big fan of bananas unless they're shoved inside a banana pudding. I'm not sure what that says about my palate, but hey, we all have our flaws. There are, however, no flaws in this recipe. The perfect amount of sweetness in the custard along with an incredible light and airy meringue make this banana pudding a real winner.

For the Pudding

⅓ cup (41 g) all-purpose flour

1 cup (200 g) sugar

¼ tsp salt

3 large egg yolks, whites saved for the meringue

2 cups (480 ml) milk

1 cup (240 ml) evaporated milk

1½ tsp (8 ml) vanilla extract

1 (1-lb, 14-oz [850-g]) box vanilla wafers

5–6 ripe bananas

3 tbsp (45 ml) melted unsalted butter

For the Meringue

3 egg whites, reserved from the custard, plus 1 more

1 tsp vanilla extract

½ tsp cream of tartar

½ cup (60 g) confectioners' sugar

To make the pudding, combine the flour, sugar and salt in a large, heavy-bottomed saucepan. In a large bowl, lightly beat the egg yolks and whisk to combine with the milk and evaporated milk. Whisk the egg yolk mixture into the dry ingredients. Place the saucepan over medium-low heat. Stir constantly until the custard is thickened and begins to coat the back of a spoon, about 10 minutes. Remove from the heat and stir in the vanilla and melted butter.

Arrange the vanilla wafers on the bottom of a 2-quart (2-L) baking dish. Slice the bananas and place them on top of the vanilla wafer layer. Pour about one-third of the pudding over the wafers and bananas. Repeat the layering process, ending with a layer of wafers. There should only be a few vanilla wafers left, so make sure to use all of them on the last layer unless you want to be fancy and save a few to crumble on top.

Preheat the oven to 325°F (165°C).

To make the meringue, in a large bowl, combine the egg whites, vanilla and cream of tartar. Beat with a hand mixer at high speed until soft peaks form. With the mixer still going, add the confectioners' sugar, 1 tablespoon (15 g) at a time. Continuing beating until smooth, glossy, peaks form. Spread the meringue evenly over the banana pudding in fancy little patterns. Bake for 20 to 25 minutes, or until the meringue is lightly browned.

BLUEBERRY HAND PIES

It's not the exact recipe, but it's as close as I could get to the blueberry cobbler my mother used to make when blueberries were in season in the summertime. The tapioca in the filling made it such that it was part pie and part blueberry pudding sandwiched between a delicious "cobbler" crust. This recipe is tweaked just a bit to make them handheld in case, you know, you need to eat a couple of pies on the go.

For the Piecrust

1 cup (226 g) salted butter

3 cups (375 g) all-purpose flour

½ tsp salt

½ cup (120 ml) ice water

For the Pie Filling

5 cups (740 g) fresh blueberries

1 cup (200 g) granulated sugar

2 tbsp (30 ml) freshly squeezed lemon juice

½ tsp cinnamon

¼ tsp salt

5 tbsp (70 g) unsalted butter

3 tbsp (24 g) ground tapioca granules

1 tsp vanilla extract

For the Egg Washes

2 eggs, beaten with 2 tsp (10 ml) water, to seal the pie

1 egg, beaten with 2 tsp (10 ml) cream, to brush the top

To make the piecrust, cut the butter into ¼-inch (6-mm) cubes and place in the freezer. Add the flour and salt to a food processor and pulse for 8 to 10 seconds. Add the cold butter cubes and pulse until the mixture resembles coarse crumbs. With the processor running, add the water a couple of tablespoons (30 ml) at a time until the dough begins to clump. Cut in half, and then form each half into a ball. Flatten each ball into a 4- to 5-inch (10- to 13-cm) disk, wrap in plastic wrap and refrigerate for at least 30 minutes before rolling.

Preheat the oven to 375°F (190°C).

To make the filling, place the blueberries in a medium stockpot and bring to a boil. Once boiling, reduce to a simmer and add the sugar, lemon juice, cinnamon, salt and butter, and cook over medium-low heat for 5 minutes. Turn off the heat and let it sit for 1 minute. Add the tapioca and stir to combine. Turn the heat to low and simmer for 10 minutes, stirring occasionally and breaking up any tapioca clumps that might form. Remove from the heat, add the vanilla and let it cool for 20 to 25 minutes.

Transfer the dough to a lightly floured surface. Roll out one dough ball until it's about ⅛ inch (3 mm) thick. Cut out rounds with a large cookie cutter. Brush the outer edge of the rounds with the egg and water wash. Place 2 to 3 tablespoons (30 to 45 ml) of filling in the center of the dough. Fold in half, and press the edge with a fork to seal. Place on a parchment paper–lined baking sheet. Repeat with the remaining dough and filling and place the baking sheet in the fridge for at least 20 minutes.

Brush the pies with the egg and cream wash. Place in the oven on the middle rack and bake for 15 minutes, or until the tops are golden brown. Remove from the oven and transfer to a baking rack to cool. Once cooled, place in your shirt pocket, purse or anywhere you might desire to have a pie.

SAUCE AND SPICE

As you've noticed throughout this book, different sauces, spices and stocks can really go a long way in either developing or rounding out the flavor of a dish. The right stock instead of water can easily take a dish from 0 to 100, and the right condiment can help bring out or balance the flavors you're trying to achieve in a dish. Here you'll find just a few of my favorite little helpers that can take a tasty dish and turn it into something phenomenal.

MAPLE BOURBON SAUCE

I serve this sauce with the Chicken and Brown Butter Sweet Potato Waffles (page 80) and also when I sell my sweet potato pies, and the response is always "gimmie more sauce!" It's so simple yet so incredible, I'm sure you'll find multiple uses of your own for it.

½ cup (114 g) salted butter
1 cup (240 ml) maple syrup
1¼ cups (300 ml) whipping cream
2 tbsp (30 ml) bourbon

Add the butter to a small saucepan over low heat. Once the butter has melted, add the maple syrup, cream and bourbon and increase the heat to medium-low. Simmer for 5 minutes, and then remove from the heat. The sauce may be kept in the refrigerator in an airtight container for up to 2 weeks.

ALABAMA WHITE SAUCE

I was a bit late to the white barbecue sauce game, but I made up for it with this delicious recipe. This sweet and tangy sauce adds a great balance to the smoky flavor of grilled meats. This sauce is used in both the Pecan Smoked Chicken with Alabammy White Sauce (page 47) and Avocado Toast with Pecan Smoked Chicken (page 87).

1 cup (240 ml) mayonnaise

¼ cup (60 ml) apple cider vinegar

1 tbsp (14 g) brown sugar

3 tbsp (45 ml) orange juice

1 tsp horseradish

2 tsp (10 ml) brown mustard

½ tsp Worcestershire sauce

½ tsp black pepper

¼ tsp cayenne pepper

¼ tsp garlic powder

Whisk errythang—the mayo, vinegar, sugar, orange juice, horseradish, mustard, Worcestershire, pepper, cayenne and garlic powder—in a bowl until smooth. The sauce may be kept in an airtight container in the refrigerator for up to 2 weeks.

CINNAMON HONEY BUTTER

I made this butter to pair with the Sweet Potato Bread (page 15), but I love to make it just to have around the house. A quick pat on your morning toast and it goes from dry to fly.

½ cup (114 g) salted butter, room temperature

½ tsp cinnamon

3 tbsp (45 ml) honey

Add the butter to a small mixing bowl and mix with a hand mixer until light and fluffy. Add the cinnamon and honey and continue mixing until incorporated. This can be covered and stored at room temperature for up to a week.

SHRIMP STOCK

YIELD: 1 QUART (960 ML)

Stock, stock, stock, stock, stock. Always a great way to add flavor to your recipes. I added this one because shrimp stock doesn't take as long as chicken or beef, but I highly recommend always having various stocks on hand. Be careful though, as you will have to play around a bit to see which recipes require full stock and which work best with a water and stock combination.

1 head garlic, sliced in half

1 medium onion, quartered

2 celery ribs, roughly chopped

1 medium carrot, roughly chopped

2 bay leaves

1 tbsp (15 g) creole seasoning

Shells from 2 lbs (907 g) shrimp

2 qt (2 L) water

Place the garlic, onion, celery, carrot, bay leaves, creole seasoning, shrimp shells and water in a large stockpot and bring to a boil. Once boiling, reduce the heat to low and simmer for 10 to 30 minutes, depending on how rich you want your stock. Once done cooking, drain through a colander or strainer and let cool. The stock can be kept in the refrigerator for 3 days or frozen for 3 weeks.

BLACKENING SPICE

YIELD: ½ CUP (60 G)

I am a big fan of mixing your own seasonings. Why? For one, buying spices from the bulk section is probably one-fifth the cost of buying it in the jar. Also, it allows you to dictate exactly what flavors you want to come through in your recipe. Control is key if you want consistency in how your recipes taste.

2 tbsp (14 g) sweet paprika

4 tsp (24 g) salt

1 tsp onion powder

2 tsp (5 g) garlic powder

1 tsp cayenne pepper

2 tsp (4 g) freshly ground black pepper

1 tsp dried thyme

1 tsp dried oregano

½ tsp poultry seasoning

Place the paprika, salt, onion powder, garlic powder, cayenne, pepper, thyme, oregano and poultry seasoning in a bowl. Mix to combine. Keep this in an airtight container and store it in a cool place.

SECRET TARTAR SAUCE

This little number is a classic example of how just a little pinch, a little scootch, can sometimes go a long way. Just how I like to switch up the seasonings in my breading for different types of seafood, manipulating the sauces can also have a great effect. Here, just a dash of cinnamon adds a tasty and unexpected flavor to this tartar sauce.

1¼ cups (300 ml) mayonnaise

½ tsp minced garlic

½ tsp paprika

2 tbsp (17 g) chopped capers

1 tsp Chesapeake Bay seasoning

1 tsp chopped fresh dill

Zest from ½ small lemon

⅛ tsp cinnamon

Mix the mayo, garlic, paprika, capers, Chesapeake Bay seasoning, dill, zest and cinnamon in a bowl to combine. This sauce will keep in an airtight container in the refrigerator for up to 2 weeks.

CREOLE BUTTERMILK RANCH

Buttermilk ranch is cool and all but sometimes you need something a bit jazzy to go with the flavor profile of the dish. Unlike your typical ranch, this sauce adds ricotta for an extra little twang, mayonnaise to help smooth it out and then hot sauce for a nice kick that brings all the flavors together. Enter Creole Buttermilk Ranch.

¼ cup (62 g) ricotta

½ cup (120 ml) buttermilk

¼ cup (60 ml) mayonnaise (I prefer Duke's)

¼ tsp garlic powder

¼ tsp paprika

¼ tsp cayenne pepper

1 tsp hot sauce

½ tsp freshly cracked pepper

Place the ricotta, buttermilk, mayo, garlic powder, paprika, cayenne, hot sauce and pepper in a bowl. Whisk together until smooth. This sauce will keep in an airtight container in the refrigerator for 2 weeks.

RESOURCES

https://undiscoveredcharleston.com/2012/06/05/the-disappearance-of-hot-water-cornbread/

https://ushistoryscene.com/article/slavery-southern-cuisine/

https://www.washingtonpost.com/lifestyle/food/how-sweet-potato-pie-became-african-americans-favorite-dessert/2015/11/23/11da4216-9201-11e5-b5e4-279b4501e8a6_story.html

ACKNOWLEDGMENTS

To my partner in crime and the love of my life, Sandra Clark. It wasn't always easy. As a matter of fact, it was never easy thanks to our rambunctious toddler. Thank you for the back rubs and encouraging words and for aimlessly wandering the streets with our son, trying to keep him occupied while we turned our living room into a photography studio.

To Rambo and Timothy Elliot. I enthusiastically agreed to do this having no idea what in the hell I was getting myself into. Without your support, vision and guidance this would not be possible.

To my sister, Sharon Iglehart. Thank you for all your support and guidance throughout this process.

Thank you to Page Street Publishing for believing in my ability and for your guidance and patience throughout this process. Thank you for trusting my creative process and allowing me to think outside of the box to bring my vision to life.

ABOUT THE AUTHOR

Chef Scotty Scott is a personal chef, recipe creator, cooking video director and owner of Cook Drank Eat, a social media platform and catering service. He resides in Fort Worth, Texas, with his partner, Sandra Clark, and their son, Mathias Woodward Scott.

INDEX